Rooted and Branching:

Women Worldwide

Dorothy Yoder Nyce, Editor
Laurel Voran, Artist

Published by:
Dorothy Yoder Nyce
1603 S. 15th St.
Goshen, IN 46526

Library of Congress
Catalog No. 98-090557

ISBN 0-916035-85-9

Printed in United States of America

Acknowledgements

- This book is dedicated to **Bessie King Yoder**, the editor's mother, mentor, and resourceful friend. A graduate seventy years ago of Hesston College, Kansas—the college her mother Anna Smith King had initiated—she continues to write speeches that others enjoy. If Bessie does not have an event to attend, flowers or garden produce to water or process, or guests in her home for a hearty meal, she reads. The local newspaper and church periodicals assume priority, but biography, history, or resources to broaden worldview also hold her attention. May *Rooted and Branching: Women Worldwide* bring her due honor, at age 92.

- Seventeen **writers** notable for global involvement and local roots deserve sincere thanks for sharing their keen insight through poetry and prose. Women whose stories are told also warrant appreciation.

- The ink drawings created by **Laurel Voran**, a trained freelance artist and professional gardener, enriches this collection. To co-produce a resource enhanced by visual affect always provides pleasure; to benefit from Laurel's artistic skill in settings of worship has also been profound. Thanks.

- A debt of appreciation is also due for **John D. Nyce's** computer know-how and persistence in following a manual or working through technical snags. Marriage of thirty and more years is thereby complemented.

- **Kathleen Fernando Peiris**, while pursuing her Masters in literature at the University of Illinois—Chicago and keeping up with young son Achal, is to be thanked for reading the manuscript proofs and for being sales manager, with the editor in India.

- **Photo and art credits**: Mary Yoder Holsopple/Gogo; Judge Mookodi/ Botswana baskets from western Ngamiland (a postcard); Janet Umble Reedy/Vietnamese widow; the editor; Gretchen Nyce/batik; Kazuaki Saitou/head sculpted in bronze. (The editor wishes to know who took the photo, given to her years ago, that appears with Samarth's article.)

Foreword

Melanie A. May

This raising up of women's voices is an instance of insurrection. Insurrection for the sake of the resurrection of our corporate and individual bodies.

We women have learned all too well lessons of blurring or minimalizing or objectifying our own differences. We have learned how to scrutinize and stereotype one another. We have learned how to steal and subvert our personal, racial, cultural, sexual, generational, physical, creedal and class particularity. In learning all these lessons, we have colluded in the crafting of a complete and totalizing identity of woman.

And so these voices of and about women resist this repressive regime and its strategies aimed at centralizing, controlling power. These women speak and tell stories in order to understand, appreciate, and honor one another's unique status and experience. These women speak and tell stories in order to conquer the myths and counter-myths that serve reigning powers and principalities.

This insurrection is not a strategy about which these women speak. This collection is itself a strategy. And the women who write are its practitioners. Not only with what they write, but how they write. A daring tangle, indeed tumult, of forms and genre is threaded through this collection. It is a tumult that heralds a new creation.

And so this collection is also an invitation to resurrection. As we conclude the Ecumenical Decade: Churches in Solidarity with Women, with the refrain "Who will roll away the stone?" reverberating all around, these voices ask us to imagine a new community. That new community, in which alliance and coalition and solidarity are possible-- hopefully fruitful--across heretofore-divisive boundaries, engages our imagination. Such a new community is not yet "real." And we dare not assume that it is latent in any biological or cultural artifacts now available. The new community is a resurrection body. A body in which we women are woven together by our divergence, yes, and even our disagreement. For the new community that is a resurrection body is set free from the bonds of our fear of conflict as of difference, by truth-telling in love.

"Who will roll away the stone?" We will, chorus the women writing insurrection and resurrection in these pages. And may the women of future generations join the refrain.

Preface

Clearly, women's stories and experience express theology. This collection of articles metaphorically depicts threads of women's theology as principal parts of a tree--roots, trunk, and branches. From different world contexts, women sow and develop distinct insight; friendships across cultures lie embedded, then bud and burst into bloom.

Rooted combined with *branching* suggests movement in multiple directions. It connotes both foundation and freedom to unfold. It endorses the hidden and the visible. Dependent on elements of water and air, on shafts of light and mute nutrients, the imagery unearths itself. So too, will articles penetrate depths or stretch their canopy when brought together with imaginative titles.

This book informs readers about specific women and experience common to women. Its organization emerges from Gayle Gerber Koontz's lead article that taps into the imagery of trees alongside the framework of theology. Phrases from hymns or general quotes related to trees [selected by the editor] head each piece. Just as verification of where a tree's roots end and its trunk begins or what demarcates a trunk's life force from that of major branches cannot be exacted, so too with categorizing stories. As readers consider whether an article depicts trunk theology more than branch or draws strength from roots, not trunk, the metaphoric stance of any contribution expands.

Rooted and Branching, through lives of real women, promotes the "coming to speech of the community of women." It values women's expression; it recognizes and honors experience as a key source of authority, as bridge for the spiritual. Writers and those written about affect identity for readers. All choose to both reveal and hide. Susan Waugh said of personal narratives: "Writing and reading about the lives of ordinary women can be 'occasions for learning and teaching, for imagining a better world, for respect and for love.'" (*Cross Currents,* Spring 1988)

Readers will learn from this volume, for good teachers practice their art. Perhaps readers will renew their motivation to create more humane local or global environs. For, what a person imagines or creates, based on accounts told by others, may lead to reconstruction of one's own context. Perhaps cross-cultural friendship will deepen, as tolerance for difference establishes new roots. And, perhaps, conduits for practicing theology will enlarge, based on a broadened worldview.

This book gestated for several years. The 1988-1998 World Council of Churches' Ecumenical Decade--called Churches in Solidarity with Women--provided incentive for global connecting. While the 1975 International Year of Women, plus the UN Decade that followed, failed to adequately influence the Christian church, women have worked for change for decades. Women named Kathleen Bliss, Henriette Visser't Hooft, Sarah Chakko, Madeleine Barot, Brigalia Bam, Pauline Webb, Connie Parvey, and Mercy Amba Oduyoye. During the current Decade, attention centers on the plight of women worldwide. As women shape their identity beyond prescribed limits and foster a spirit of communion beyond loyalties of nation, denomination, or faith, solidarity will grow.

Newspaper headlines highlight global realities. "Women Seek to Eradicate Racism (Brazil)." "Thai Woman Works with Poor." "Maternal Education on the 'Roof of the World' (Nepal)" "Nun Tells Rape Story (Guatemala City)." Articles here further disclose the human story. As writers introduce a particular friend, describe activities or explain circumstances, readers do well to trust an author's authority. Writers choose what to reveal or expose. They respect distinct cultural features. They stand rooted in content while also branching into visionary hope.

Diversity lies inherent. The number of years each writer lived within a culture not hers by birth varies. All have pursued graduate degrees. Those in sociology, literature, or population study complement the majority with seminary degrees. Writing styles vary; my intent was not to impose uniformity. Poetry appears, notably from Jean Gerber's creative mind. And Laurel Voran's ink drawings augment the creative voice. Story heroines include an author herself and representatives of cultural groups. An account of women's bringing about social change in Colombia and a case study from Zambia appear along with disciplined research into abortion in Japan and a noted Indian novelist.

As the Decade of Churches in Solidarity with Women concludes, how we anticipate the flowering of women's roots, trunks, and branches in the century ahead could enhance the practice of theology.

Dorothy Yoder Nyce
Goshen, Indiana

Table of Contents

1   *"...But trees were different in different places."*
                           Marjorie Kinnan Rawlings

Theology from the Roots

Gayle Gerber Koontz

A colleague in the Philippines, Everett Mendoza, with whom I taught a theology course, once said that theology is like a tree. Theology is carried on at several levels--at the roots, in the trunk and in the branches. That metaphor caught my attention. Later, while thinking about forms of theology in my own Mennonite denomination, and specifically about women doing theology in the two-thirds world, the image of the tree re-emerged as a way of visualizing distinctions between and connections among the various forms of Christian theological reflection.

What counts as "theology" continues to be a matter of definition and debate. An appealing aspect of the metaphor of the tree is that it includes a wide range of theological activity. Yet it allows for distinctions between forms of such activity. Further, rather than emphasizing competition and struggle for power--inevitable when drawing lines between those who are and are not doing "real theology"-- the metaphor illustrates the significance and contributions of root, trunk, and branch reflection to the work of theology as it seeks to sustain and renew the Christian church.

Therefore, I prefer a broad definition of Christian theology, something like "a critical reevaluation and constructive appropriation of the Christian tradition we have received on the basis of the best knowledge available to us from all sources."[1] Given this definition we might expect the most sophisticated or comprehensive features to emerge from the branches of the theological tree. However, theological reflection emerges at any level where Christians use the best knowledge available to critically evaluate and adopt the faith tradition they have received. Key here is the word "critical." It assumes some effort to see the tradition clearly and truly in order to exercise judgment that is as careful and fair as possible. Whether or not any particular judgment is *sufficiently* critical is a basic question. It is precisely why theologians at root, trunk, and branch levels need each other.

Theology at the Roots

Christian theology at the roots refers to critical evaluation and adoption of the Christian tradition carried on by those who have not had formal theological education beyond what is available through regular channels within a congregation or parish. It is usually oral rather than written. If written, it may be handwritten, mimeographed or copied, or shared among friends or the local congregation. It is not formally published or made public.

Such theological reflection may be embedded in new songs written for congregational worship. It may occur in prayers and family devotions; in Bible studies at women's meetings; in diaries and journals; in children's stories that teach about God, Jesus, or the church. It may emerge in informal discussion at church camps, conferences, or in college dorm rooms. Small group Bible studies which include interpretation and reflection about how God is working in the lives of members may exemplify "root theology." It may surface at congregational meetings where members seek to understand faithful choices for Christians on varied issues: refugee assistance, finances, conflict, healthy sexuality, or response to government policy.

Theology at the Trunk

Theological reflection at the trunk level can be more sustained and self-critical than at root level. Trunk theologians usually have some formal theological education beyond the congregation, or they have found and used additional resources for biblical study and interpretation, for understanding church history and culture. Bible College graduates, university Bible or religion majors, or those with seminary level study may become trunk theologians.

People who reflect theologically at the trunk level often hold positions of leadership in the church. These may be pastors, Christian educators, denominational staff, editors of church papers, or missionaries. They may or may not perceive of themselves as "theologians." Theology at the trunk level is often written and is published or made public in some form beyond a local congregation.

Such theological reflection might be exhibited in or serve as the foundation for any of the following: sermons, including those transmitted by radio and television; hymnals or other songbooks; religious drama; a cookbook designed to teach responsible eating for those with choice; adult Sunday school lessons; conference or denominational statements on such issues as human sexuality, leadership and ordination, or Christian participation in revolution or war; articles in church papers and magazines; classroom lectures on Christian faith; meditation guides; fiction or nonfiction written from a Christian perspective.

Theology in the Branches

African theologian Mercy Oduyoye suggests that branch level theology is done by those who are "competent in writing, analyzing, evaluating, and criticizing theological works."[2] Theological reflection on Christian tradition at branch level can be done in a highly self-critical and systematic way. It assumes awareness of the scholarly theological disciplines and the ability to employ the arts of these disciplines: biblical and historical knowledge, research and interpretation; cultural analysis and evaluation. Such theologians have formal theological education and are likely to have vocations as teachers, writers, missionaries or other church leaders or have enough wealth to pursue this work in leisure time or retirement. Such theological work is usually developed in sophisticated theological language and presented in lectures or conferences and/or published in scholarly journals or books.

The Theological Tree

A tree is an organic unit. The image of a theological tree reminds us that theological reflection occurring at different points in the life and work of the church are part of a larger whole. Three of my convictions are that 1) each of the levels of doing theology makes valuable contributions to the life of the church; 2) all levels need to remain connected in order for each to be spiritually alive and faithful to the God of Jesus Christ--to remain sufficiently critical; and 3) trunk level theology is critical for the life, health and mission of the church because it connects with both root and branch theology.

Normally when we talk about theology, we mean branch theology and when we use the term theologian, we mean professional or academic theologians. Other theological speaking and critical evaluation among Christians is by definition invisible. Theology is what certain scholars do; it becomes real theology when it appears in print. By definition theology at the root and trunk levels is silenced.

From the perspective of a branch theology that defines itself as the only legitimate or real theology, there is only silence at the roots. And theological voices that surface at the trunk level are likely to be discounted as shallow. From the perspective of root theology on the other hand, the jargon at the branch level is nearly impossible to understand and it is difficult to see how sophisticated theological debates make any difference in real life. They are so much noise.

I am acutely aware of the problems that arise when branch, trunk and root theologies are disconnected. Examples of such problems might be drawn from a branch theological response to a televised sermon or a root feminist critique of traditional theology.   But I wish to cite examples from a book by Niall O'Brien, *Revolution from the Heart,* itself an example of trunk theology.[3] Niall O'Brien is a Catholic priest who lived on the other side of Negros, the island in the Philippines where my family and I lived for two years in the late 80's.

O'Brien began his work in the Philippines soon after Vatican II. He was excited about the new developments and committed to reform Roman Catholic liturgy and spirituality, given the new guidelines. While he was alarmed by the poverty he saw, it did not disturb him deeply since he felt his work was ministering to the soul. A turning point for him occurred when he walked for several days to a new parish in the farthest village to which he was assigned. He took food along for the way but not enough for the whole journey.

> I had taken shelter from a passing tropical shower in a shack several hours into my journey. In the hut were some adults and some children. The children were bloated from what I now know was lack of food and probably infestation with intestinal worms.   The children had no clothes except for T-shirts.
>
>   I took out my food and was thoughtlessly beginning to eat it when I noticed all eyes upon me. It dawned on me that they were all hungry and there was no food. I shared what I had, regretting that I had not brought more. The adults refused, allowing the children to take it, and the children wolfed down the little I had to offer, making me ashamed that I had begun to eat without thinking of them in the first place. I had often fasted, but this was the first time in my life that I had experienced hunger because there was no food.[4]

This incident disturbed O'Brien more than he realized. He later felt he had unconsciously made the decision from that moment to support anything that would bring the Columban missionaries closer to the poor.

Gradually O'Brien began to walk with the poor in a new way. He moved to a house open to the life around him rather than continuing in the parish house upstairs which kept poor people at a distance. He began development projects, learning from his failures, and went with hacienda workers to owners to report that the workers were not making enough money to buy basic clothing.

He also began to read Scripture with new eyes. He saw that Christian theology, if it were to speak to the majority of the people in his parish, had to speak of God in relation to the economic sins that kept them hungry and ill.

He remembered hearing Pope Paul VI speak briefly after a charismatic flavored worship service in Manila.

> You have tasted the fruits of the spirit. Now you must do the *works* of the spirit. The people of the world need life. They need bread!" Bread: he had said the vital word for me. food: not just spiritual food, but bread, rice, beans, for hungry stomachs and outstretched hands....
>
> Those words of the Pope renewed my spirit and helped me shake off some of the melancholy that had kept returning so relentlessly these last few years. That melancholy came from the conviction that all the magnificent cathedrals of the world, the stained glass windows of Chartres, the Book of Kells and all the illuminated manuscripts, the Cistercian monks singing the "Salve Regina" in their evening stalls, the nuns in perpetual adoration before the Holy Sacrament, the Sistine Chapel, and even the "Exultet"--all the great works of the Christian spirit--were but ashes, for one simple reason: we were Dives and Lazarus was at our gate, waiting and waiting for the crumbs from our groaning table.[5]

As O'Brien began to listen to root theologians in his parish, the word "community" took on new meaning. He saw that it was not just for those who joined orders. But ordinary church people shared, made decisions, took risks in working for justice, prayed together, sought reconciliation, and built community.

At the same time his own theology at the trunk, influenced by study of branch level theology, challenged forms of tradition that were blindly accepted at the root level. For example, O'Brien was convinced that to change the traditional way of handling payment for sacraments was important. He felt the sacraments could never have their full spiritual and human meaning as long as they were caught up in commerce. In his next parish assignment the first thing he did was to refuse all payment for funerals and services for the dead.

In his former parish the poor, who he had seen walking along the road carrying coffins, never brought their dead to be blessed. At first the same was true in the new parish. But as they realized that no financial embarrassment would follow, that changed. After awhile no one passed by; he would often come home to find twenty people sitting silently beside a coffin. O'Brien's theological perspective changed his practice, which affected the practice of parishioners, which left space for deepened meaning of the sacraments at the level of root theology.[6]

Another way to describe this is that trunk and branch theology can draw on the perspective and tools available to them to help shape a tree that is faithful to God's revelation in Jesus Christ. At the same time, no branch level theology can remain vital for the church--for people doing theology at the root level--if it does not voice and evaluate Christian tradition in response to questions and convictions emerging at the roots. We do not all speak theologically in the same manner or with the same breadth, depth and angle of perspective. We need each other.

Third World Women and Theology

The theological perceptions of third world women--many of whom are poor and suffering--have been almost entirely ignored, until recently, by formal or branch theology in the western world. This is partly because the majority of theological reflection by third world women, done at root and trunk levels, is not readily available to intellectuals in the north and west. But it is also due to lack of interest and attention, that is, to sexist attitudes and structures that affect both women and men in many cultures.

Before the late 1960's women's voices were virtually absent from the arena of branch theology. Since that time, numerous women have sought theological education, challenged androcentric theological assumptions, and made creative contributions to biblical interpretation and theological vision. However, if we limit our theological gaze to the critical reflection that takes place at branch level, we will continue to find little theology by women from Africa, Asia, and Latin America or by women of color in North America.

If we widen our definition to include root and trunk theology, we will see many more ways in which theological reflection by women in the two-thirds world are stimulating further critical evaluation and appropriation of Christian faith. To illustrate, I offer an example of root/trunk theology from Latin America. In a simple study guide for

International Women's Day in Ecuador, a mother reflects on a drawing made by her six-year old daughter. The child's sketch shows Jesus on the cross--with a smile, breasts and a wide skirt.
"She gave it to me on Easter," the mother remembered. "I confess that I cried a lot after seeing it. So many things passed through my mind that my heart overflowed with cries of happiness and sadness. I asked my daughter for an explanation of the drawing."

> "Who is it?"
> "Well, mommy, it is Jesus of course," looking at me as if I were silly and incapable of recognizing it.
> "Hmm, and why the smile?" I insisted.
> "Mommy, you have taught me that Jesus loves us and died for us. Jesus is smiling because of that love," Raquel answered.
> And she left, tired of my silly questions.
> I remained crying and visiting with God. First, I asked if God had seen the drawing.
> "Of course."
> Then I asked other more direct questions:
> "Who is this woman?
> What image of man and woman is my daughter developing within her?
> Who does she believe to be in Christ's place?"
> Questions without answers.[7]

This personal root level reflection became the basis for a branch level, published lesson guide focusing on the Lamb of God and the crucifixion of Jesus in relation to women and men in church and society. Such theological reflection no doubt stimulated more root level review of Christian scripture and tradition among women in Ecuador. It may or may not have reached the attention of other trunk or branch level theologians in the country.

Root and branch level reflections by women in the two-thirds world have been collected and published reflections on biblical texts in *New Eyes for Reading;* articles in the Asian magazine *In God's Image*; stories which illustrate some African women's "root" theologies in *Surviving Without Romance*; The WCC publication *Ecumenical Decade 1988-1998: Churches in Solidarity With Women*; a collection of Hispanic women's essays edited by Ada Maria Isasi-Diaz and Yolanda Tarango.[8] But many untapped resources remain.

Although the majority of two-thirds world women who critically engage Christian tradition do so at root and trunk levels of theological reflection, we must note that two-thirds world women also "do" theology at the branch level. Mercy Oduyoye from Ghana, Virginia Fabella from the Philippines, Chung Hyun Kyung from Korea, Elsa Tamez from Costa Rica and others do engage at this level. Many are members of the Ecumenical Association of Third World Theologians (EATWOT).[9]

Mercy Oduyoye reports that in New Delhi in 1981 women began to cluster because they felt they were not being taken seriously enough in EATWOT. Earlier, only men presented papers and led meetings. Sexist jokes were told in public sessions. The women responded by initiating a Commission on Women. After women theologians worked together on the national level and then by continents, there was an Intercontinental Conference, "Doing Theology from the Third World Women's Perspective" in Mexico in 1986.[10]

In 1990 when Oduyoye visited the seminary where I teach, one of the students asked her, "Why are there so few third world women doing [branch] theology?" She responded that women are indeed theologians and that they are writing. Literature, at this point, is mostly limited to essays in journals. Often it is not circulated outside of the woman's own country.

Publishing theological books in the two-thirds world is difficult. "Who is going to buy the book?" she asked. "Who can afford it?" Third world publishers concentrate on educational textbooks that they know will sell. Further, educated women in Africa usually teach in universities as part of the government educational system; seminaries are less likely to hire women. Because of their university context, teaching and research tend to be focused in Islam and African religious traditions and their relationship to Christianity. Scholarly projects focused on Christian theology proper have to be done "on the side"; most governments do not consider theological writing a high priority for funding.

Further, third world women with theological education often focus their energies within their own country rather than attempt to speak to an international group of colleagues. "It's enough to try to understand things in one's own country, rather than trying to understand and write for outsiders," Oduyoye points out.

Also, the few theologically educated English-speaking women theologians who live in the two-thirds world are overextended. They need to write, lead the church, and teach or mentor women in their own countries. For example, the Circle of Concerned African Women Theologians in Ghana consists of women in theology, sociology and literature who work with women's groups in the churches. They belong to local groups and volunteer to lead Bible studies.

In the Philippines I saw the weariness of a female faculty colleague who teaches full-time. In addition, she counsels many students, travels every weekend to supervise pastoral interns or visit graduates, frequently preaches and attends or speaks at church conferences. She also feels responsible to write and edit educational materials and a monthly newsletter for the Philippine Association of Women in Theology. In terms of the theological tree, third world women who might write branch level theology often give priority to working with and among trunk and root theologians.

Perhaps for this reason, they are well prepared to express in the arena of branch theology the questions and insights of two-thirds world women whose own reflection takes place at root and trunk levels.

Theology from the Roots

Third world women critically evaluating and appropriating Christian tradition at root, trunk and branch levels raise questions for all of us. They trouble and enrich our theological reflection. As Mercy Oduyoye puts it in her essay, "Who Does Theology?," when

> nonacademics have been recognized as 'lay theologians,' more gifts are brought to the service of doing theology. Their participation has already called us back to the springs of doing theology--faith, experience, action.[11]

She also points out that when theology at the branch level listens to and responds to root theology,

> the language of theology ceases to be obscure and mystifying, for it becomes a communal venture, ... it is a construct of the people, not an attempt to understand some classic theoretical formulation of the faith.[12]

There are at least three areas that third world women theologians from the three continents address in common: problems of religion, gender and culture; biblical interpretation; and some specific issues in theology and ethics.

1.   Theological reflection by two-thirds world women frequently addresses questions of sexuality, religion and culture in particular countries. They express how women look at these. They evaluate what

is positive and negative for women in these cultures, and in Christianity as it has developed there. That a woman theologian in Africa would reflect on attitudes toward and the rights of widows in traditional law and in Christianity is not surprising.[13] Likewise, a Filipina who cites more egalitarian male-female relations in traditional culture asks how this challenges (especially Spanish Catholic) Christianity built on a male-privileged system.[14] The report of the intercontinental third world women theologians conference in Mexico notes that for women from all three continents "theologizing emerges as a way in which women struggle for life--arising from experience of being discriminated against or used as women and as people of the third world."[15]

For this reason theology at the branch level by third world women theologians has a distinctly feminist character. Kwok Pui Lan from Hong Kong writes that feminist theology

> will be a cry, a plea and an invocation. It emerges from the wounds that hurt, the scars that hardly disappear, the stories that have no ending. Feminist theology in Asia is not written with a pen, it is inscribed in the hearts of many who feel the pain, and yet dare to hope.[16]

Nevertheless, in a 1985 consultation of Asian women, Indian representatives noted that the women's struggle in the Churches of India has not gathered momentum. Korean women theologians report that most churches shun social concerns. Even Filipino theologians who are involved in GABRIELA, a strong and organized women's movement, recognize that the largest church in their country--Roman Catholic--continues to reinforce a conservative view of women. Third world feminist branch theology may genuinely emerge from the suffering of third world women, but it remains a prophetic voice.

2. Third world women theologians have given energy to rereading the Bible from their social and cultural perspectives. They ask questions such as "How is the Bible read in most churches?" "Is that what the biblical writers truly intended?" "Is the Bible for or against us?" Most branch level theology looks for interpretations that are liberating to women bound by poverty and prejudice.

The report of the intercontinental conference in Mexico indicates that

> in Latin America the poor have rediscovered the Bible and, in it, the liberating God. This has allowed women,

who are part of these poor and oppressed, to capture the spirit of the text while distancing themselves from the letter. . . .In Asia where Christians are a minority, the Bible is read in the concrete context of life struggles and of interfaith dialogue. In Africa, there is a marked trend of a conservative reading of the Bible.[17]

Third world women theologians agree: to highlight Jesus' relation to women and his counter-cultural stand with respect to women is important. Like their northern and western counterparts, they look at biblical texts from the standpoint of their own experience as women or from that of the women involved in the text.

Mercy Oduyoye notes that if a man from African culture talks about Jesus, he likely talks about power over the waves, over death. He is not likely to focus on Jesus' relationships to women or on biblical stories from the woman's point of view.   In interpreting the annunciation, for example, male third world theologians have usually focused on God's turning the world upside down ("the rich will go empty away," from the "Magnificat"). Oduyoye would focus on the feelings of Mary: what were and are the cultural blocks that prevent women from saying yes to God?[18]

3. A primary theological issue for women in the two-third's world is Christology. And it has significant import for ethics. Oduyoye says that one African Christology focuses on the paradise to come, on future African unity. In African cultural values, anything that gathers into a whole is good; what is outside the circle is bad. With that emphasis there is a tendency to forget other strands. For example, the gospel will also bring conflict and divide families. Or, for the sake of the gospel, to challenge tradition might be appropriate.

Christology is also linked to attitudes toward suffering. One theme that runs through the branch level reflection by women in various countries asks: "Is it okay for women to struggle and resist the evil of sexism?"   That leads to discussion of theological views that undercut and undergird this.

4. Third world women theologians also highlight specific ethical issues. Faith and poverty, economics and power are critical issues for third world men as well as for women. Women theologians express how poverty and hunger especially affect women. Women and health is another priority issue for ethical action: more than half of all women in developing countries--230 million--suffer from anemia. Other critical

areas for Christian ethical reflection include economic and physical exploitation of women in industry, household work, and sex tourism; militarism, war and women; and, in many settings, the powerlessness of and limitations placed upon women in the church. Women in the two-thirds world raise theological and ethical questions for the churches in their own countries as well as for Christians worldwide. They also offer theological directions that make sense in relation to their lives and contexts. These questions and directions call for additional theological reflection at trunk and branch levels in the worldwide church. Then Christian theology, at its most informed and self-critical levels, can articulate a vision of God and world that, among other things, is truly healing, saving, just, and loving for women in the two-thirds world.

Endnotes:

1. This definition is slightly modified from Maurice Wiles quoted by Mercy Oduyoye, "Who Does Theology: Reflections on the Subject of Theology," *Doing Theology in a Divided World,* ed. Virginia Fabella and Serges Torres, (Maryknoll, NY:Orbis, 1985), p. 145. [Words in the brackets are mine.]

2. *Ibid.* p. 144.

3. Niall O'Brien, *Revolution From the Heart,* (Oxford:Oxford University Press, 1987).

4. *Ibid.,* p. 17.

5. *Ibid.,* p. 62.

6. *Ibid.,* p. 125.

7. Casal, Rev. Jose Luis, ed., "8 De Marzo Dia Internacional de la Mujer" (Quito, Ecuador: CLAI, Pastoral de Familia, Mujeres y Ninos, 1991), informally translated by Linda Shelly.

8. John Pobee and Barbel Wartenberg-Potter, eds., *New Eyes for Reading,* (Geneva:World Council of Churches Publication, 1986). Mary Lou Cummings, *Surviving Without Romance: African Women Tell Their Stories* (Scottdale, Pa.:Herald Press, 1991). *Ecumenical Decade 1988-1998:Churches in Solidarity With Women* (Geneva:World Council of Churches Publication, 1988). Ada Maria Isasi-Diaz and Yolanda Tarango, eds., *Hispanic Women: Prophetic Voice in the Church* (San Francisco:Harper and Row, 1988).

9. An important introductory collection is *With Passion and Compassion* edited by Virgina Fabella and Mercy Oduyoye (Maryknoll, N.Y.:Orbis, 1988). Also see Elsa Tamez, ed., *Through Her Eyes: Women's Theology from Latin America* (Maryknoll, NY: Orbis, 1989.)

10. Mercy Oduyoye spoke to the class "Women/Men: History and Vision" at the Associated Mennonite Biblical Seminaries, Elkhart, Indiana, in the fall of 1990. These and subsequent comments were made during that class session.

11. Mercy Oduyoye, "Who Does Theology?" *Doing Theology in a Divided World*, p. 148.

12. *Ibid.*

13. Mary Lou Cummings, *Surviving Without Romance*, pp. 160-61. See footnote 8.

14. See Sr. Mary John Mananzan, ed., *Woman and Religion* (Manila:The Institute of Women's Studies, St. Scholastica's College, 1988) as well as her essay "Redefining Religious Commitment in the Philippines Context," *We Dare to Dream*, ed. Virginia Fabella and Sun Ai Lee Park (Hong Kong:Asian Women's Resource Centre for Culture and Theology and the Asian Office of the Women's Commission of the Ecumenical Association of Third World Theologians, 1989).

15. From the report of the Intercontinental Conference of Third World Women Theologians initiated by the Women's Commission of the Ecumenical Association of Third World Theologians, Mexico, 1986.

16. (Kwok Pui Lan quoted in *MCC Women's Concerns Report* (Akron, Pa.: Mennonite Central Committee, May-June 1987, p. 11).

17. Report of the Intercontinental Conference of Third World Women Theologians initiated by the Women's Commission of the Ecumenical Association of Third World Theologians, Mexico, 1986.

18. Oduyoye's comments here and in the following paragraph are from the class session referenced in footnote 10.

2

*"...That's part of me there, walking along.
Tree from which I sprang."*

Shirley Ann Grau

Gogo: The Unsung Heroine

Mary Yoder Holsopple

Gogo Khelina is a woman of strength--hardworking, weathered, thin but of sturdy build, capable and barefoot. She is the heartbeat of the family. Gogo Khelina is the "grandmother" who holds the family together at our adopted Swazi homestead.

Gogo, the Siswati word for grandmother, is the term used when addressing an older woman. Gogo of this story is an ordinary woman, one less likely to get recognition for her work compared to one who holds a "powerful" position. But she is always busy. Tough-skinned yet vulnerable--which is true for anyone who lives a hand-to-mouth existence.

She is even partially toothless. But because of her ready smile and hearty laugh, I had never noticed that her front teeth are missing. As I tried to get her to relax for taking her photo, she laughed enough to reveal the truth. She became self-conscious, almost ashamed.

Matriarch of our adopted Swazi family, Gogo is the mother of five daughters and a son, plus the grandmother of many grandchildren. Just how many grandchildren live with her varies--generally hovering around nine or ten. Whether some are children of her sister's children is uncertain to me. That I cannot count the grandchildren is good; to know the number may bring them bad luck.

For adult children to take their baby to a mother's homestead to be raised is common practice in Swaziland. Some are left because born to a daughter but not recognized by the father as his. Some children will remain for years while others stay only during school holidays. This solves childcare needs and frees a mother to pursue employment in towns or cities. The *gogo* expects this; the practice seems to cause no animosity.

Therefore, who happens to be in residence at any particular time is indeed fluid. Therefore also, Gogo easily accommodated our family of four when we moved in with her for two months at the beginning of our MCC (Mennonite Central Committee) assignment in Swaziland. People come and go according to needs--financial, physical, or emotional. Gogo is always there, to provide what is needed.

She is as steady as a rock. Since her husband left her to marry another woman (also common practice in Swaziland) years ago, she has been the breadwinner, decision-maker, and caregiver. Gogo decides what to plant and where. Gogo provides the school fees for her grandchildren. Gogo carries the babies on her back while she goes about her work.

Gogo was assigned a particular piece of land by the Chief, acting on behalf of King Mswati III. In rural areas individuals cannot own land except for a few large, private farms held mostly by white Swazi's. Two-thirds of Swaziland is Swazi national land.

A Swazi homestead is a collection of huts that make up one family. Gogo's homestead is dug out of the side of a mountain. The odd-looking line of mud and wattle huts has grass thatching and/or rusting, iron sheets held in place by huge rocks. Each hut is a different "room"; each serves a different purpose. One is used for storing agriculture equipment--hoes, hand-powered maize mill--one for the chickens, one for making and storing the current handicraft project.

One hut is reserved for each adult member of the family. In addition to Gogo and an alcoholic brother, these include her adult son Dumisani and his "wife" and newborn baby. Two of Gogo's adult daughters and their children are also there, plus on occasion another daughter. Another hut is for an "uncle." But in all my time there, I never met him. Nor was that hut unlocked.

One hut is for cooking. The floor of the "kitchen" is smeared weekly with cow dung to keep it fresh and clean. In the winter Gogo cooks over an open fire surrounded by three rocks, on the kitchen floor. At night she and her youngest grandchildren sleep there to absorb some of the warmth of the cooking fire. In the summer Gogo cooks on her wood stove. Collecting firewood is a daily task, generally assigned to several older grandchildren. Water is collected from the marsh down the mountain.

In Swaziland, women become part of the husband's "property" when they marry. They move to his homestead, plant his fields, give birth to his children. Three of Gogo's children have moved to their husband's homesteads. Two stay with Gogo; their "husbands" visit sporadically. They do not provide financial support for their "wives" and children. Homesteads typically include only women and young children.

Men, fortunate enough to have a job, are employed in urban areas or the mines of South Africa. Gogo's son recently moved back to the homestead from a paraurban area. He had lived there while working as an unskilled laborer for a company that was later liquidated. This now leaves Gogo to figure out how to meet the needs of her growing brood.

She works hard. She plants her fields with maize, pumpkins, and beans. She also uses local grasses to make handicrafts--floor mats, market baskets, and all-purpose handbags. The beautiful, braided floor

mats are for a door size or an entire room. She also makes *emancansi*, the traditional sleeping mat that is easily rolled up to carry. She sells these crafts wherever possible—mostly to people who come to her homestead since she has no transport to take them to market.

Gogo is also a woman of faith. She frequently visits the sick. She is an active member of a Zionist church--the Christian Catholic Apostolic Holy Spirit Church in Zion. Zionist churches in Swaziland are part of the African Independent Church "movement." They do not rely on western missionaries to import or interpret the Bible for them.

Christianity is contextualized. Priorities make sense. Even though people of Gogo's church are quite poor, they will find food for a hungry person, a place to sleep for one who needs it. Community is very important. When someone is ill, the religious community gathers to assist. They pray. They often hold all-night services in which praise, penitence, petition, and preaching are combined. They function as a priesthood of believers whereby anyone who feels "led" may preach during a worship service--impromptu style.

Community people often come to Gogo when they need healing. She combines traditional ointments, teas, and herbal remedies with fervent prayer and faith. She is a gentle woman, one who is not afraid to touch people. To see her is to see God at work, even though she is an illiterate, uneducated woman.

Is this woman to be pitied? Her life is hard, without a doubt. She has many responsibilities. But when I look at Gogo, I see a woman of strength. Her eyes sparkle. She is loved by many and revered by her children and grandchildren. Most importantly, she has an air about her that says she is at peace with herself and her God.

May her kind of assurance permeate humanity. May those like her know that their story is worthy. Gogo Khelina!

3

"O Holy Spirit, Root of Life"
Hildegard of Bingen

Pregnancy and Birth

Linda Witmer

Pregnancy: To Dread or Celebrate

While recently visiting one of my Kekchi[1] friends in Guatemala, she shared her story. Listening, I gained a deeper appreciation and admiration for the multiple qualities of strength of these women.

Maria's story is fairly typical. Sitting in her home, I recalled the harshness of life for Kekchi women. However, she represents less than one percent of Kekchi women who can read. Her husband Juan helped her learn.

Further, Maria and Juan share a more equal relationship than most couples. Open to new ideas, they use local medical services. And he recently honored her desire to stay at their present home, near her family, rather than move back to his home area.

During the past ten to fifteen years Kekchi people settled in northern Guatemala. One of twenty-eight indigenous groups within Guatemala, they know oppression from the ruling Spanish class. For example, two percent of the people own eighty percent of the land.

Land in this new frontier was given to the people to clear and settle. Although promised, no official titles were ever issued. Many established communities were later moved by wealthy people who bought the land or by foreign oil companies (including U.S. owned) that took the land for drilling. Maria and Juan have been resettled twice. They now occupy a small plot of land, without a title, near the town of Las Casas.

[Note: Two stories from Kekchi women/couples in Guatemala, one from Marie's view, the other expressing the writer's views. Names are changed to protect the privacy of families.]

As I listened to Maria's story, she busily worked in her two-room, ground floor, thatched-roof home. Ducks she raises waddled in and out of the house while we talked. Maria's mother-in-law occasionally added her thoughts.

While Maria prepared a typical meal, I sat in the kitchen on a stool. She stirred black beans on the fire table, ground corn, and patted tortillas for our lunch. She seemed to enjoy sharing her story, a story neither unusual nor unique among women. Every so often she sat down on the bed near her two-year-old, mentally retarded child. She comforted and talked to him before returning to her work and this account.

"I was 12 years old when Juan came to my father and asked to marry me. Much to my relief, my father told him, 'No.' I was not thinking of marriage. I wanted to stay in school and learn to read.

"Then my father broke his leg. Since walking was difficult, he was restricted from working. This handicap limited family income and, therefore, resources for food.

"Juan came back about seven times to talk with my father. I overheard their discussions but was never asked my opinion. They finally agreed on our marriage.[2] I was one less mouth to feed. The two men negotiated the date when I would move to Juan and his widowed mother's house.[3]

"My father took me to Juan's home. I waited outside for awhile, not wanting to go in. Finally, I had the courage to enter. I became his mother's helper and learned how to keep house her way. His father had died of alcoholism when Juan was a year old.

"Our religious backgrounds were different. Juan was a member of the Kekchi Mennonite (Protestant) Church, while my parents and I were steeped in Mayan traditions and beliefs.[4] My grandfather was a traditional healer. I had been taught to fear Protestants. Strange stories were told about them. For example, pastors supposedly had many wives.

"Everyone assumed I would become a Christian when I married Juan. Although I was baptized and became a member of the church, I never really believed in this new faith. I rarely prayed. I kept wishing to return to my traditional beliefs and customs. Even after Juan became the pastor of the local church, I continued to struggle with a choice between the two religions.

"At age 13 I became pregnant. We were not accustomed to using modern medicine. We knew little about delivering babies, and there were no local midwives. Getting to the nearest hospital involved a nine-hour bus ride over bumpy, dirt roads. So Juan and his mother helped me with the delivery. Our baby boy lived only a few hours.

"In less than a year, I birthed another baby boy. About a month before the due date, I fell. The infant was born premature; he too lived only a few hours. After his death, Juan and I were very sad and discouraged.

"Following the delivery, I had heavy bleeding for days. I didn't eat or drink. I became dehydrated. I felt very weak and couldn't get out of bed. In desperation, I asked Juan to call a traditional healer to come to perform a healing ceremony. This angered Juan. He scolded me, saying that we don't believe in the evil powers of the healers.[5]

"I was afraid I was going to die. I began to think about and question my faith in God. I wondered what God might be trying to teach me. Then I began to pray, to ask God for help. Church members fasted and prayed for me too. After that, I felt a little stronger and drank a gourd full of water. Through this life-changing experience, I had a new understanding of the power of God in my life. I wanted to serve God with all my heart.

"After I had regained strength, I walked to the new clinic of the Kekchi Mennonite Church. The nurse advised us to wait to have children until I was stronger. I took birth control pills for several years.

"Juan was sad that we had no children. His mother told him to leave me and find a wife who could give him children. Juan told me he would wait to see if our next child lived. If not, he would look for another wife.[6]

"In a few years I stopped taking the pills and immediately became pregnant. I was scared throughout my pregnancy, fearing the baby would die. I prayed and fasted. A healthy baby boy was born. Again I was strengthened in my faith. God honored our prayers. Juan and I were very happy.

"We decided I should take the pills again for a few years. Three years later I stopped taking the pills because of headaches and high blood pressure. I became pregnant again. My fears of pregnancy returned. Further, I really didn't want to be pregnant. During this pregnancy, I developed a form of rash all over my body.

"We decided to go to a nearby town for prenatal care with a Spanish-speaking doctor. I don't speak Spanish but my husband knows a little. The doctor scolded me for not coming earlier. He warned that the rash on my body would pass through to my unborn baby.

"We were also told that we needed to choose between my life or the baby's life. Or, the doctor suggested that I fly to the nearest hospital for an operation to remove the baby from me. We were confused and didn't know what to do. We couldn't afford the very expensive plane trip. The doctor wanted to call the plane for the following morning. Juan and I kneeled to pray for God's intervention. Although unexpected, I went into labor during the night and delivered another baby boy. We both lived! This was another sign of God's goodness to us.

"The baby was very weak and had a body rash. He was slow to breast-feed. I manually expressed breast milk into his mouth. Slowly he gained strength. But something seemed wrong. He didn't develop like my other child.

"The clinic gave him vitamins and told me to stimulate him as much as possible. They advised that the more I work with him, the stronger he will become. But he will never be normal, whatever that is.[7] By the age of two, he could walk by holding on to things, plus say a few words. I am encouraged by his progress.

"God has been very faithful to me. I feel very fortunate to have two children. My difficulties during my pregnancies have helped me to grow in faith, to depend on God for strength."

Our conversation was interrupted when Juan returned home from a church committee meeting. With beans and tortillas ready, the local village health worker joined us for lunch. Maria continued patting tortillas in the kitchen; she served us while we ate. Juan beamed as he spoke of his children.

Several weeks after this visit, Maria confided her news of being pregnant again. She expressed considerable fear, not convinced that she welcomes the prospect.[8] The question lingers, What might transpire during the coming pregnancy?

-----

*Notes

1. The Kekchi people are the second largest indigenous group in Guatemala. Each group speaks a different language and has distinct dress. Women wear a gathered skirt--eight yards of heavy, hand-woven material--tied with a drawstring. They wear a simple blouse with a half-slip under it; this is easily flipped up for breast-feeding.

Most Kekchi average about five feet in height. Features include olive skin, brown eyes, high cheekbones, and a rounded face. Their black hair, parted in the middle and formed into a braid in the back, includes a bow.

2. Patterns change. Whereas fathers used to decide about marriage, mothers as well as daughters now enter discussions.

3. Marriage often does not begin with an event. (A civil marriage and a wedding ceremony in a Catholic or Protestant church increasingly occurs, however.) The two begin to live together, usually in the husband's house. He usually provides a

dowry, sometimes giving gifts several times. Just before the two become a couple, he gives a black skirt and white blouse. The wife serves the mother-in-law and learns how to make tortillas.

4. In common thought called "acuas," a child who sees or smells any of the birth process will get sick. People believe in the hot and cold theory. Certain illnesses need hot medicines or food, others cold.

Pregnant women and pregnant animals are also thought to be "hot," which means to have evil power or a strong spirit. They can cause sickness, (as can my strong spirit, being from North America). A child can reveal symptoms of a weak spirit--to not eat, and become anemic or malnourished. This often occurs when breast-feeding stops (at two years) because the mother is pregnant again.

5. Protestants often discredit the ceremonies and special powers that traditional healers evoke. Healers vary; some use herbs while others do not. Depending on the diagnosis, rituals are performed over a sick person. For example, with "susto" an egg is passed over the body.

Presently, herbal medicines are more accepted. Our health promoter classes include them, and a noted, elderly Protestant woman prays to God and uses many herbs with people who come from great distances to seek her traditional healing.

6. Expressed by Christians young in their faith, this would not have been a common solution. Principles of loyalty to one wife and the importance of children remain strong here.

7. The child is Mongoloid. Only a few mentally disabled children survive here, likely because of poor care. (I've seen only two Mongoloid children in eleven years.)

8. Although change occurs, the culture expects couples to have many pregnancies. Children come when they come. When half of them died, women birthed more often. Now that more live, women assume the freedom to express the desire to limit births. While male children know preference and privilege, girls are needed to help the mother--to grind corn, make tortillas, and help care for other children.

Birth—a Holy Moment

An unexpected, "holy moment" describes my being with a Kekchi friend for the birth of her first child. Mixed emotions surfaced. She was afraid. So many Kekchi women die in childbirth. What could she expect? No one prepared her for the birth process. She feared the pain-- how long would it last? Would she have strength to endure it? Many details could go wrong. Would the child live? Would she have a retained placenta? Would she hemorrhage? With an infant mortality rate of eighty-four and a half per one thousand in the rural areas and a maternal mortality rate of eleven out of every hundred, Juanita had reason to fear.

Only her family, with their knowledge from attending births, could assist her. Fear of the unknown loomed large in the house as labor began at 5 p.m. For a first birth, the pregnant woman's mother often helps. For later births, the mother herself delivers her baby, sometimes with the help of her husband.

Juanita and Pedro live with Juanita's parents, a common custom. Seventeen years old, they live in a typical two-room, thatched-roof home with an earthen floor and pole walls.

Visualize the kitchen. A shelf holds a few dishes, clay pots, and tin cans for cooking. Three large stones on the ground hold the pots over the fire. A tin can of coffee brews over the fire, ready to serve family and guests. A grinding stone on a narrow table mashes the lime-soaked corn for making tortillas, the staple of the Kekchi diet. A few stools and one small table for serving food stand nearby. Most family activities occur in this one room. A divider separates the kitchen from the bedroom.

I found Juanita lying on a wooden bed with a reed mat, her mother beside her. Both looked apprehensive. They asked me to examine Juanita, to report on the progress of labor. I had only a stethoscope. I was conducting home interviews in the community, not there in the role of a nurse.

Contractions occurred at ten-minute intervals for about two hours; then they stopped. At about midnight with labor unchanged, I suggested that we go to bed. Juanita's grandmother agreed to sleep there in case the process resumed. Having delivered her daughters' children, her knowledge was respected. Clueless about my expected role, I wondered who was in charge--grandmother or me.

At 4 a.m. Pedro nervously called for all of us to wake up. Contractions had started again; the bed revealed that the water had broken. Grandmother directed activities. Plastic sheets were stretched along the outside walls to prevent wind from entering cracks and to keep people, notably children, from seeing the event. Kekchi people believe that children are vulnerable to sickness, or may even die from seeing or smelling any part of the birth process. Household children went elsewhere to sleep.

Pedro dug a shallow hole in front of the room divider. He put a piece of clean plastic over it, plus paper on top of the plastic. He leaned a large wooden pole at a forty-five degree angle against the room divider above the hole and tied it firmly. When the time to push arrived, Juanita would squat over the hole under the pole, holding on to the pole for support.

A small fire smoldered nearby, to keep the mother and infant warm. It would prevent cold air from entering the mother's body during labor. Pedro brought in a bed built for the occasion--thin poles tied together with rope to be placed across low logs by the fire. While Pedro completed his tasks, I counted Juanita's contractions, taught relaxation breathing, and encouraged her. The contractions resumed ten-minute intervals.

Intending to hitch a ride on a truck in the morning, I agreed to stay with the family for the delivery. However, no one explained her expectations of me. Wishing to be sensitive to cultural practices and the grandmother's expertise from having delivered more babies, I waited for instructions. I did request clean rags, a string to tie the cord, and a new razor blade. No blankets or clothing had been purchased for the new baby.

Labor progressed slowly. I used my stethoscope to listen to the heartbeat. When I gave everyone opportunity to hear it, Grandmother's

response surprised me; she easily distinguished the sounds. Fascinated, all felt relieved to know that the baby was alive. With stethoscopes often seen as instruments of magic, to have family members listen to the heartbeat dispelled some of that magic.

Everyone waited. Juanita seemed to tire by about 10 a.m. Others wondered about such a long labor. Grandmother and I assured them that it could continue. Pedro's parents also arrived in the morning. We all sat in the kitchen with Juanita, talking and waiting. I remained fairly quiet and listened to their words of advice. We spent time in prayer--asking for God's protection for both the mother and infant.

Some expressed concern that Juanita should be pushing. Grandmother directed Juanita to squat behind the pole and to begin pushing with each contraction. Thinking that she might tire and concerned that she conserve strength for later, I suggested that she might wait until she had bearing down sensations. Then the labor stopped.

Exhausted, Juanita asked to lie down. Quite a discussion followed about the wisdom of her lying down. After agreeing to place the bed over the logs, Juanita slept for about half an hour. When she awoke, I suggested that she walk around the room. Soon the contractions became regularized and Juanita squatted behind the pole. Pedro supported her on the one side and her father on the other. Apprehension showed on their faces. She pushed with each short but ineffective contraction.

I began to feel the vulnerability of Kekchi women. What would we do if something went wrong? She might need a C-section, begin to hemorrhage, have a retained placenta, or develop another complication. Being a day's trip from the nearest hospital and without emergency or regular transport (the last truck of the day had gone by), we knew no doctor to call.

Accustomed to more technology, resources, and options, I had no equipment or medicine. Reliant on my education and knowledge, I felt impotent and weak. Present with this family, I knew their vulnerability. We depended on God, little else. We prayed for protection.

What happened next surprised me. I left the room for a few minutes. Suddenly, (at twelve o'clock noon) I heard an infant's cry. I was told to pick up the infant, a role I had expected Grandma to have. Juanita's wide, eight-yard skirt obstructed my view. But under the skirt on the plastic sheet lay a crying newborn in a pool of blood.

I gathered the slippery little girl into my arm, asking for some cloths to clean her. An old, but clean, T-shirt was given. Squatting beside the mother, I held the newborn and waited for the string and razor. Grandmother instructed me not to cut the cord until the placenta was delivered. They believe the cord will return inside the mother and get lost. While in an uncomfortable, squatting position for what seemed like a long time, I held the child. Soon the placenta expelled and I cut the cord. (Later, I explained that the cord could be cut prior to the delivery of the placenta without causing harm.)

Juanita lay down on her bed beside the fire. Given a basin of water and soap (no washcloths or towels), and seated on a low stool by the fire, I washed the infant while everyone watched. Fearful that I might proceed inappropriately, I expected both grandmothers to give advice. With the bath completed, I handed the baby to great-grandmother and attended to Juanita.

No one seemed concerned about her or noticed her profuse bleeding. I massaged her abdomen and explained the importance of that action. I also asked for more rags. Without sanitary napkins, the rag supply had also been depleted.

Meanwhile great-grandma took care of the baby. After loosely wrapping a clean cloth around the cord, she had wrapped the newborn in a clean cloth. Placing the arms to the sides and the feet together, she tied narrow strips of cloth at the waist, knees, and ankles. This is believed to help the body grow straight. Not using clothes or diapers, only a cap donned the newborn's head, to prevent cold air from entering the body. Such air would cause sickness. The fontanel is generally treated with special care; remedies keep the fontanel from sinking into the baby's head. When grandma (now great-grandma for the first time) finished, the baby resembled a little mummy.

The first breast milk, colostrum, believed to be unhealthy, is not given to the newborn. Understanding their beliefs, I still recommended that she be put to the breast at once. They agreed with my remedy, to reduce the mother's bleeding.

The new mother needed no coaching to breast-feed. She seemed like an expert. To everyone's surprise, the baby began to suck at once. Among the Kekchi, children are usually breast-fed for two years or until the mother becomes pregnant again. They believe that breast milk acts as poison from a pregnant mother, for her body is very "hot."

Pedro buried the placenta and blood lost during the birth process. Then he bathed and changed all his clothes. Considered contaminated, blood from birth or menstruation can cause others to become sick.

Pedro then brought in a chicken he had killed for the special feast. Both grandmothers prepared the meal. The custom of eating a spicy chicken or turkey soup following birth gives the new mother strength. Thought to be "hot," the mother's body needs a cooling food like chicken. The Kekchi classify illnesses as either hot or cold. Foods eaten and treatment prescribed must correspond with the illness.

Everyone sat around the fire and chatted happily. The other children returned home. We all enjoyed a delicious meal around 3 p.m.

The remainder of the evening was spent in the kitchen. Juanita and her baby lay contentedly near the fire, and Pedro attended to his wife's needs. Juanita's bed will remain in the kitchen by the fire for forty days, to avoid cold air from entering her body. To rest also helps her gain strength.

For approximately one month, the baby is called a "little cat." Then, or at baptism when named, she becomes a person. This custom likely reflects awareness that a child may die during the first month. Even after naming the child, people often call her by a nickname because of her weak and vulnerable spirit. If the god of the mountain hears the child's name, the god may call the child to itself, causing the child's death.

Seated around the fire, Pedro began asking about Jesus' birth. "Do you think Jesus was born in a similar way as my baby?" he asked eagerly. We discussed the setting of Jesus' birth. Perhaps their setting had advantages over Jesus' grotto. It must have been dirty or smelled of manure because of the cattle in the stable. All alone, Mary and Joseph had no family to help and support them.

Jesus' birth took on new meaning for me. Born of oppressed people like the Kekchi, he also arrived during political instability. Mary and Joseph likely feared childbirth; at that time, many women died in the process. Inexperienced in delivering a child and with no medical resources, the young couple's child appeared. With a stable less than sanitary, an open fire glowed on the dirt floor, similar to that in Pedro and Juanita's home. Surely Mary and Joseph felt vulnerable or knew fears during labor and delivery. Utterly dependent upon God, their faith that God controlled their situation sustained them.

This was a "holy moment" for me. A precious memory of a learning experience lingers. Being present with Kekchi friends--to experience their fears, feel powerless, and then celebrate the birth of a healthy baby--was a gift to me.

As we celebrated life that evening, another Kekchi family in the same village mourned. Due to a retained placenta, a mother died in childbirth. The woman could have been Juanita. I realized anew life's fragility. And so I choose to be present with Kekchi women's suffering, to offer hope.

I believe in God's presence. With all seemingly stripped away--God IS--in the ordinary, in the celebrations, and in the crises. Although the mystery and wisdom of God surpass me, I know and rejoice in God's faithfulness, love, and hope. My Kekchi friends have drawn me to both deeper faith and more profound appreciation for the tenuous quality of life

4   *"I like trees because they seem more resigned to the way they have to live than other things do."* Willa Cather

DORCAS'S STORY

Mary Kay Burkhalter Larson

Background for Case Study

Dorcas (age 36 in 1991) asked that I assist her in thinking about her future. She had left her husband for about a week in order to get perspective or "fresh air" as she said. She came with her youngest, seventh child who was still breast-feeding.

I had intended to write stories of several Botswana women. As I reflected on Dorcas' story, I saw many themes common to African women whom I have known.

The deteriorating economic situation in many African countries often gets told in country-level statistics but rarely at the household level. Dorcas's account of life at home, as the copper prices dropped in Zambia, was indeed poignant. As an African woman emerging from traditional roles, she has trained as an accountant and held formal employment.

However, she remains constrained by traditional roles through social interactions and community expectations. Marriage comes relatively early. Family size is large and obligations to the extended family remain heavy. How the common person experiences victimization through collapsing infrastructure and poorly-trained personnel becomes clear by superficial understanding of motor mechanics and failing medical care. Women of childbearing age and their children under age five are especially vulnerable to these weaknesses in national services.

In addition to being victim of physical and emotional violence in the home, Dorcas was hostage to a legal system. While ostensibly present to protect her interests, in fact, it proved to be a vehicle for further abuse. Migration in search of work and more freedom grows as a theme in modern Africa, demonstrated in Dorcas's story as her family takes up employment in neighboring Botswana. However, in these situations the male usually receives the work permit while the spouse struggles to obtain one.

I asked Dorcas if I could record her story with my intent of writing it for others to read. Dorcas told her story in English. I have attempted to retain her authentic words. Names have been changed to protect the identity of the persons involved.

FOR LOVE OF MY CHILDREN
Childhood and Changing Family Fortune

I am from a family of eight children. There were some years between me and my older sister. My mother thought that maybe she wouldn't conceive any more. But one night she had a dream that my father was giving her a white chicken, which is a blessing. So that month she conceived me.

When I was young, my father was working for a contracting company, Frank Fergerson. He was a carpenter and a builder. When Frank Fergerson closed his contract in Zambia, he handed my father over to his friend who owned a bakery. My father worked there six months.

Then he said, "Let me use this money that I was given at the end of this contract." So he opened up a business. He was mending shoes, repairing bicycles and radios. He had one helper. My elder brother was also helping every afternoon, after coming from school.

And then we were doing gardening a lot. Gardening was there all along. So when my father started that little business, he asked the local Council to allow him to open a small shop. We bought our first truck--a Toyota 6000--for eleven thousand *kwacha*. Later we bought a Datsun for three thousand *kwacha*. He bought them for cash. We started living a very comfortable life. I could have anything that I wanted. I had a lot of friends because my father was well-off. Our friends didn't have a fridge, but we did. We were using an electric iron, a stove, a three-plate cooker. We were quite comfortable.

But we continued going to the garden as we used to. We didn't have a maid or servant. I used to do washing, especially for my mother, and we used to take turns selling at the shop. I would go in the morning and in the afternoon my young sister would come. We used to close the shop at 9:00 at night. It was busy. Over the weekends we would work together, the two of us. Early in the morning, at 5:00, we would go and sweep and arrange things and start receiving deliveries. Milk and bread was being delivered early in the morning--6 a.m.--so we had to be there. Also, Coca-Cola and Fanta were being delivered to the shop.

About 1978 or 1979 things began changing in Zambia and my father's business started declining. The deliveries stopped. We had to go to the milk depot to buy it. Maybe after standing for three hours in the queue, we could buy only one crate of milk. There was often a shortage.

They would say, "No, we have run out of milk. Come tomorrow."

One day we had a problem when a baker came to borrow my father's vehicle. My father was busy going to church and these people came to ask if they could rent the truck.

So he said, "Okay, but I want you to hire my driver."

They said, "No, when we hire vehicles, we use our own drivers."

He said, "No, I can't allow that."

Off he went because he was going to church. After he had gone, they used their own driver. When they started off, they didn't check anything. They didn't check water; they didn't check oil. The engine was damaged before they even reached the place where they went. Then they had to come back and report to my father.

He said, "You go and take the vehicle to get it repaired."

But it was not repaired. The vehicles started getting damaged one by one. Spares were scarce. So the vehicles kept on standing and standing until now it was out of hand. Bush mechanics came to steal parts from my father's vehicles. They would come in the night. They would take one wheel off. They would take the windscreen or whatever they wanted. That is how he collapsed.

I said to him, "Why don't you sell this vehicle?"

He said, "I can't. If I sell it, how will I manage to buy a new one?"

And then my mother started getting ill. She was experiencing problems.

Meeting George

When the business completely collapsed, I was already married. We just went straight into marriage. I was seventeen or eighteen. I didn't know him. It was my friends who knew him.

I said, "I don't like him--the way he dresses and the way he walks."

My friends said, "It is better to marry a person who looks like this. You won't be happy with that other boyfriend of yours because he is handsome. He'll give you problems so better marry this shabby man.

Dorcas, you like fancy things and you will change him. He will look the way you want."

So, of course, I started changing him. I said, "Why do you dress like this? You should dress like that. You shouldn't eat in public. You shouldn't eat very much. You should always change shirts at least once every day. Comb your hair after work."

He used to work in the *abbatoir* (slaughterhouse). When he would remove the head cap, the shape of the cap would remain and he would go to the bar like that. But after he changed, I brought problems to myself. He started seeing other girls.

Problems

The problems started very early. They began when I was expecting the second child. I didn't realize he was seeing other women. I couldn't believe it. I was a Christian girl. I respected tradition. When he would come home in the morning, I would ask, "Where did you go?"

He would say, "Oh, last night I got very drunk and I slept at my friend's place."

So it went on for one year. Still I thought he was with his friends. But my friends started saying that he was always with a certain girl, and that they were holding hands. That is when I began opening my eyes. So that is what he goes to do! I never knew in my life that a man of God could do that. I was brought up in a decent home. My father and mother didn't quarrel. They could differ over money because my mother also started her own business. But they would come together when it came to banking or buying something very big. That's the life that I knew.

Now I was expecting the next child because the babies were coming one after another. I would conceive when the babies were eight or nine months old. Let me tell you about when the third one was born. The labour pains had already started. I had heard what George was doing. That night he came home at 11:00 p.m. I asked him to look at the time to see how often the labour pains were coming. I take long, so usually I don't rush to the hospital. Usually, I take nine or ten, sometimes twelve hours. I would only go to the hospital when the pains were about ten minutes apart. In the process of timing the pains, he fell asleep because he was drunk. I tried to wake him. I even slapped him, but he didn't wake up. I decided I had better leave.

It was about a 30-minute walk from our house. On the way I felt the baby coming down. Then I stood for a while and I said, "No, I won't reach the clinic. I must go back home." So I went back. I started slapping him because in our tradition he shouldn't be there when I start delivering. He woke up and left. I started preparing myself to deliver. He went to the neighbors, but they didn't wake up. I had to call my young sister. She was doing Form II (ninth grade). She delivered me. George phoned the mine police. Usually if you tell them that it is a maternity case, they bring a nurse with midwifery training. When the midwife arrived, she saw the baby already born.

Then I told my young sister, "Don't mention it to anyone." It's not proper in our custom for someone who is not married to deliver. I had told her what to do. She was very young.

I remember the time that my next child was born. George had said to me, "Let me go and buy milk for the baby. I'm coming."

So he went. He came back and he found his boyfriends watching me in the bedroom. So he said, "Okay, I'm coming."

With that he was gone. That was 2:00 in the afternoon. The following day I never saw him. I said, "Where is he?"

My neighbors said, "No, let this man go. This is not the way to behave. It is better to just go."

Then I got on a bus and went to my mother. It was forty kilometers away. I arrived in the afternoon around three and I found that my mother was at church. When she came back around 6:00, she said, "Now have you come to visit?" And then I explained to her.

So she said, "No, you should have waited for him to come. You cannot leave in his absence. What if he is killed? People would say that you have arranged to get him killed. If he is out, it is better for you to wait for him and then you come."

So I was in the process of explaining when George appeared. He didn't say anything. He was just silent.

Traditionally my father is not to discuss anything like that with him. It would be considered obscene. My father said to him, "You can go out with your friends to play. But you should come home early because you know that someone is waiting for you at home. So do you want to say anything to us?"

George said, "No, I just came to get my wife."

My father said, "I think I will encourage my daughter to get employment. You have taken my daughter out of employment and now she is just sitting."

When I was expecting the sixth one, I had problems again. We moved to Ndola (a mining town in the copper belt). George's family used to come often, traveling more than two hundred kilometers. There were regular buses. They would come to buy cooking oil. His sister would also come with her children and her husband. It was just too much. I told George I would have to move out. I asked him to please talk to his people. He said it was because I received them so nicely.

I told him, "How can I not receive them nicely if they come to my house? Should I just tell them that they should go back?" I was very uncomfortable.

My father usually did not come, but once he came because my young sister was very ill. The house was very, very full. I told my servant to go and sleep with his friends so my father could use his quarters. My father said, "Why do you live in such a way?"

We lived there four years. But the visits were every day. This one would come and then another. They did not write to tell us they were coming. They would just get on a bus. In our tradition, they can just come. Of course, the educated ones let you know that they are coming.

The grandfather would come. He had never been to town before. You know if someone comes from the village, we have to buy him a *chitenge* (African cotton print) and a headscarf for the wife. We also must give them bath soap, washing powder, a candle, and a blanket. So we were forced to buy all those. George tried to talk to them, but they never listened. You can tell them you have no money, but still they come.

Like recently his young brother came. The mother told the young brother to come and be firm in making his requests even if George tells them that he already has many debts. We gave him a blanket and shoes and some trousers. Then I grew so thin, like I am now. It was then that George applied for a vacancy in Botswana. That is how we ran away. We thought that there we would have fewer visits. If we go back to Zambia, it will be the same, because George is the breadwinner. He is the oldest in his family of four children. He is from a small family, unlike me.

When we came to Botswana, at the beginning I had a very good life. George used to work very much in the home. He would come home in the evening and start washing clothes for the children, and the following day he would iron them. I would clean the house and cook. We came in 1986 but in 1987 problems started.

My neighbors used to come and say, "Why is your husband always in the kitchen? Why is he always home? Why doesn't he find friends to play with?" George didn't say anything. He knows it is his job.

So one day he came at lunchtime and said, "I'm going to see a mechanic." That was all.

I saw him the following morning at 9:00 a.m. I didn't ask him. I just looked at him. And then he just continued coming home in the morning to come and bathe and change and go to the office. He said nothing. But if anything was wrong, he would shout and he was sulky. I never said anything.

Choices

Now I can't even count how many girls George has had. I used to know the number, but now I have lost count. I think it is over one hundred women. He knows about AIDS. You would think that he would change his lifestyle. My father also says, "Why does my son-in-law behave this way and yet he has been to school? Is he not afraid of these diseases?" My father gets most unhappy.

But people come from work, wash and go to the bar in the evening. Their lifestyle is similar to that of Zaire where people dance in the evening after work. Alcohol doesn't make people forget. They just want sex. If it (AIDS) happens, it happens. They say it is just one of those things.

As far as George and me, we were living in tension for a long time. Then I told him, "I can't take it anymore."

He got so much involved that it was like he was married to his girlfriend now. He came home only to wash and change his clothes. His girlfriends would spray perfume on his trousers and smear powder and lipstick all over on his shirt. But I continued to wash his shirts. When I was ironing, his trousers especially, it was awful because the perfume was so strong. I knew it. He was behaving like he just didn't care. He would come home from work, wash and go, just openly like that.

We just discussed it once and fought. That time he asked me if I could give him a chance to enjoy his life. So I said, "Okay, I'll go and you remain and enjoy your life." And I left. I stayed away for two months.

My friends then started to say, "Do you think it is a good idea to leave children behind?" Then I just didn't know what to do. I would have brought the children. My father told me to stay and forget about the children.

I wanted to leave George because he was chasing me away. He was under pressure from his girlfriend. He would come and say, "I don't like what you cook. You cook rubbish. When you prepare meals, don't even think about me."

So I said to him, "Am I forcing you to eat from here? Just buy for the children so they can eat. If you don't eat from here, it is okay. I don't mind." So that is how we continued until I left.

My friends wrote to me after I had left, "Dorcas, if you stay longer, don't be surprised to hear that one of your children is dead. We see them walking in the rain and we don't know why. The father is never there." So I came back.

Then he said to me, "Why have you come back because I am not ready for you. I didn't ask you to come back."

I said, "I didn't come back for you. I came back for the children. You continue with your lifestyle."

He said, "Yes, I'll continue because I'm not ready to stop." So he continued. He said, "Give me a chance to enjoy myself."

Once some of my friends from Zambia came on his birthday and talked to George. They said to him, "Have you lost your head? What are you trying to do? If you are confused, we should take you to the mental hospital."

Then he said to them, "You know, uncle, I know that what I have done is really bad. We have come to Botswana as guests and it is not our country. I want to change my lifestyle." The following day, there was a wedding. That was the first time we went out together. A Zambian man was marrying a Botswana woman.

After the wedding he said, "I'll be back. I won't take long." He went for good. I said to myself, "Why was he talking like that yesterday?"

My son told me that when I was away, their father would take them to a certain home in Gaborone West. They would wait in the car for ten minutes, and then their father would take them home. Their father would later return to that house. He said that he could show me the house.

Early in the morning we got a taxi and went to that house. I went to the door and asked George's girlfriend to ask him to come out. There was silence. Then he came out and he paid the taxi driver. I said to him, "George, I think it is about time that you introduced me to Julie. And after you introduce me to her, we will go to your office. Tomorrow will be your last day here. You can say 'bye-bye.' But first introduce me to Julie and explain why you are so involved with her. Doesn't she know that you are married?"

So he said, "Let's just go home." I was standing near his car. Then he told me to open the door and get in the back seat.

I said, "I can sit in front. Why should I sit in the back seat?"

So he said, "No, you get in the back."

That is when she came out and said, "You witch, what do you want at my house? Who brought you here and why are you involving children? I'm going to shoot you." She was pointing a gun at me.

Then I said to her, "You go ahead." Then a man came. I don't know if he was from the neighborhood or just passing. He passed me and went to the woman and threw her into the house, with the gun in her hands. After she dropped the gun, she came out again.

So I said to her, "Why don't you find your own boyfriend?"

She said, "I found this one."

Then I said, "You are wasting your time. Do you think you are his first girlfriend?"

George said to her, "Julie, you are causing a scene."

She said, "You are the one who is causing it."

Then that man said, "Take your wife and go." We went home.

After that experience, he stayed for about four months. That is when I gave up hope. I decided not to struggle against this relationship again. I only stayed for the sake of the children. He resumed his behavior, except now it got worse. George's girlfriend once insulted my young sister. My sister replied with insults. The girlfriend didn't like it. She shouted at George. George reacted by saying to my sister, "I don't want you. You go."

He didn't give her transport money. So she went and stood by the roadside. She explained to the truck driver that she had no money but that her uncle would pay in Zambia. That's how she traveled. I had asked her to come and stay with the children and then I would send for them. But she left.

Failure of Tubal Ligation

In late 1989 I was beginning to notice myself feeling ill. I said to myself, "What's wrong with me? I feel so much of the heat. And usually this illness comes when I am expecting." I told George.

He said, "What? You mean that when they operated, they failed to sterilize you?" He told me to go and have the pregnancy ended. I went back to Zambia and I had an appointment with a gynecologist working for the mines.

He said, "No, I am a Christian. I cannot perform an abortion. Do you really want to do that?"

Then I said, "I have nothing to say. It is my husband who has sent me here. I won't say I want to terminate, and I won't say I want to keep the pregnancy. I'm just neutral."

But then he looked at me and said, "No, you tell me the truth. Are you going to keep the pregnancy?"

I said, "I'm a Christian. My husband has forced me to come here. He says he doesn't want the baby."

He said, "I too am a Christian. There is no way I can destroy life."

I went to see my cousin whose husband is working in the mines. She advised me "Your marriage is very unstable. It is better to do what he wants." When I didn't respond, she made another gynecologist appointment.

He said, "It is already late. You are twelve weeks along. If you had come earlier, maybe I could help you. You see, you are carrying twins."

I stayed for a month and then had to return to Botswana. I said to George "I don't want to discuss whether you want me to carry the baby or not."

I went to a nearby hospital in Mochudi for antenatal care because I was told there was a good gynecologist there. I decided to deliver in Botswana because it was easier to take care of my children. When the babies were fully developed, the doctor at Mochudi asked me to stay. I told the doctor, "Doctor, the babies are breach. What do you think you are going to do?"

He knew everything about my medical history. He knew that my firstborn was 1975 and my lastborn was 1984. He knew I had labour pains for twelve hours. Labour with this one was twelve hours. I delivered two very big babies who seemed healthy. The first one was 3.7 kg (8 pounds 2 ounces), and the second one, weighed the following day, was still 3.2 kg (7 pounds 1 ounce).

The second one had suffered some distress due to prolonged labour. It was taken away and placed in an incubator. The nurses reassured me that it was fine, but I could not have the baby with me. Even the doctor would tell me nothing, though I knew all was not well. In the end, it was the nurse who told me that the second baby had died. It was such bitter news. I could hardly bear to accept the truth. In part, the medical staff was responsible. I know it wasn't my fault.

About this time George was transferred to another large town. I asked myself, "Shall I move with George or just go home to Zambia? I don't want my children to suffer directly from their father. That I don't like."

So George came and picked me up in Gaborone. When we moved to this new place, we were given a small house. Most of our belongings were outside. I moved with him because of the children. Then he started again.

He would never be new to a place. He would always say, "I'm coming. I'm coming." And he would stay for two or more hours. One day he said, "I'm coming." He went for good. He stayed Friday, Saturday, Sunday. On Sunday afternoon he came back. I didn't ask him anything. For the first time, I didn't cook for him. The children had already eaten. Around 6:00 I made myself a cup of tea and bathed. I still didn't say anything. On Monday I went to his office to explain why I had started doing this. He wasn't there.

He came home at lunchtime and said, "I have to go out on a business trip." He began to pack. He was away for five days. When he came back on Saturday, he made himself very busy. I prepared a meal for him. After he had finished eating, he washed and prepared himself to go out.

Then I took the car keys. He said to me, "This is where I leave the car keys. Where are they?"

I said, "I have them, but I won't give them to you. Where are you going?"

He said, "You have no right to ask me that."

I answered, "I want to know, because if you are going to see your women, you are going to carry all your belongings." Then I pulled down the suitcase and told him to pack. He began beating me, banging my head against the wall. Finally, I fainted for twenty minutes. Still I didn't give him the keys.

I said, "It is better you kill me rather than me give you the keys. You are going to kill me so you can see those girls. Then you can say, "The one who bothers me, I have killed her, now we are free."

Then the neighbors came and asked what had gone wrong. George said, "I wanted to check on the mail and she refused to give me the keys. That is why I beat her."

After I felt a bit better, I went to the police station. I walked with the children. When we reached the police station, I gave a statement. They said, "Where is your husband?"

I said, "He is at home."

The police went to our house and asked George to come to the police station in the afternoon. They said to him, "Your wife has come here and has complained. Is it true?"

He said, "Yes, it's true."

"Do you know that you assaulted her?"

"Yes, I know."

"Did you do it on purpose or did she force you?" He remained silent. They asked him to come back and see the Commanding Officer the following day. When he asked me to come, I told him I wasn't yet ready. He went. I walked.

The police said, "Your husband was here. What do you want us to do?"

I said, "No, you just go ahead and take him to court." Then they asked me to come back tomorrow and bring the children. So we went there the following day. When they asked the children what happened, they explained. They said that the children had to sign the statement as well.

I said, "No, that way I don't like it. I don't want the children to go to court. I don't like it. I think it will give them a bad experience."

"So, what are you going to do?" they asked.

"I will withdraw the case." That is how we withdrew it.

George is not too different from other men. His lifestyle is the same. It is just that he gets excited and reacts; that's the only difference. If I had a boyfriend, he wouldn't like it. If his daughter ran around, he wouldn't approve. He would be strict with his family but not with himself. He fails to control himself. People like George shouldn't even marry. They should stay single. These are the men you see roaming the streets when they are very old. Their lifestyle tells. Finally their wives run. They could get married twelve or thirteen times. But they don't settle. They die a very sad death.

Epilogue

Despite repeated appeals for help, no simple solutions for Dorcas exist. Her circle of friends cannot show her a way out. With no resources of her own to begin an independent life, she feels obliged to remain with George. With family in Zambia in such a precarious economic situation, she cannot move in with them. Having seven children makes that option impossible. Not a national citizen of Botswana,, she cannot find employment there. She remains with George.

[Mary Kay later wrote that the surviving twin failed to thrive and died. She led in graveside ceremonies, joined by a group of Zambian expatriates.]

5

"Tree of life, thy branches we."
Percy Dearmer

Women in the Spiritual Healing Church in Botswana

Rachel Hilty Friesen

When I first came to Botswana in 1986, I had only a few vague ideas about African Independent Churches. After interacting closely for five years with one such church, the Spiritual Healing Church, I have come to appreciate their creativity and strength. These qualities are epitomized in the lives of the women with whom I have become acquainted.

African Independent Churches, a new religious movement, resulted after Christianity was introduced to Africa in the nineteenth century. Some groups broke away from the churches established by missionaries, e.g., Anglican, Methodist, and Congregational. Others spontaneously emerged, often led by a prophet who had seen a vision and felt called to start a new church.

Other noticeable features appear. With leadership of such churches exclusively African, these groups remain totally independent of mission boards and outside funding. They have often incorporated elements of traditional African culture and religion into their worship life and beliefs in ways not usually found in mission churches.

In 1952 the Spiritual Healing Church was founded in Botswana by Prophet Jacob Mokaleng Motswaosele. A Methodist by background, Prophet Mokaleng had been a migrant worker in South Africa for two decades before his spiritual ministry began. He had the gift of healing. During the early 1950s people flocked to his home village, Matsiloje, to seek healing and other kinds of help. Eventually a new church formed. This grew into today's Spiritual Healing Church with twenty-eight congregations throughout Botswana. Prophet Mokaleng died in 1980.

The present head of the church is Archbishop Israel Motswaosele, eldest son of Prophet Mokaleng.

Women in the Church
As I visited some of the Spiritual Healing Church congregations, I noticed a greater number of women present than men, at most worship services. While the formal leadership is exclusively male, females make up the clear majority of members (as high as seventy-five percent). In a large urban congregation like the one here in Gaborone, fifty or sixty men might be present on a Sunday morning. But in a small village, two or three men might be the norm, within a congregation of twenty or more people. This prevails in part because for much of the time many of the village men work away in town or at their cattle posts.
When asked, some women gave another reason. Men do not attend church because they do not want to give up the habit of drinking beer. The Spiritual Healing Church, like most independent churches, maintains strict regulations against the use of alcohol. This strikes men at the core of an important male social activity, group beer-drinking. Among women, beer-drinking is less common and less important in Botswana society. Giving up alcohol, therefore, challenges men much more seriously than women.
Why a large number of women attend church results from the freedom of expression provided. They find opportunities for participation there. To an outsider like myself, women appear to occupy a subordinate position that corresponds with general social norms.
But others tell me that they disagree. For them, the church means opportunity. They feel that they enjoy a high degree of independence within their women's organization where men do not interfere. Many women feel that they are free, rather than oppressed, in the church. The church relies on them a great deal. Most would agree that women are "the backbone of the church" and that they "carry" the church financially, through their fund-raising activities.

Mothers' Union
The Mothers' Union originated in the earliest days of the Spiritual Healing Church. Organized soon after the church's founding by Martha Tshose Motswaosele, the wife of Prophet Mokaleng, she began to gather the women into a fellowship similar to one she had earlier been active with in the Methodist Church. Open to all women age nineteen or older, unmarried mothers (almost fifty percent of Botswana mothers) feel accepted into the Mothers' Union equally with married women. Their participation in the organization or, for that

matter, in the church as a whole, is not restricted, as it might be in a mission church.

The organization provides encouragement and Christian fellowship for women. This goal evolves through weekly Sunday afternoon gatherings and through annual conferences. The Sunday afternoon "class" includes prayer, singing, and preaching; three or four women may preach at each meeting. As far as I know, there has never been any question about women's preaching within their own organization. The Mothers' Union must obtain approval from the church's male Executive Committee for their plans, an approval virtually always given.

Church Uniforms

A characteristic of independent churches in Africa is the use of church robes or uniforms for all members, both women and men. Uniforms provide church members with an important sense of identity and belonging. Based on a vision of his, the founder usually chooses the uniform colours. To see a thousand adult members of the Spiritual Healing Church, in their striking blue and white uniforms, dance in procession through the village of Matsiloje at dawn on an Easter morning was an impressive sight.

Chosen during the group's earliest days, the uniform for this church has never changed--with one exception. Prior to 1969, the women wore a white *douk* or head covering--a long cloth wrapped around the head something like a turban. They expressed dissatisfaction with the *douk* and changed to a plain white hat.

One male member of the church told me that the women themselves wanted the change. By 1969 many independent churches had begun in Botswana. Women wore the white *douk* in virtually all of them. Since women of the Spiritual Healing Church wanted to be different, they formed a committee to take the question to the ministers. Approval for change followed at a Synod meeting.

However, a woman told me that Prophet Mokaleng initiated the change. At that time many women thought that women of the independent churches should wear their white *douks* all the time. This practice meant that the *douks* became very dirty, especially if women also tucked items (including snuff--a forbidden substance) into the folds of the *douk* for storage. The prophet objected to this custom and decided that women should wear white hats instead, and only at church.

Formal Leadership Roles

The Spiritual Healing Church designates four levels of pastoral congregational leadership: 1-preacher, 2-deacon, 3-evangelist, 4-minister (*moruti* in the Setswana language, with *baruti* the plural). Each minister must rise through these levels which serve as a form of apprenticeship. Women have not been a part of this formal hierarchical leadership, with the exception that women may be deacons. The task of women deacons mainly entails giving treatments, such as massage or baths, to women who come to the church for healing. Men perform similar tasks for other men.

At the Easter Eve service at Matsiloje, women surprised me with the freedom, ease, and spontaneity with which they spoke. Until then, I had heard only men preach in public worship services. The service began around midnight. From then until early Easter morning, one speaker after another expounded on the meaning of the resurrection of Christ. Throughout the night men and women speakers alternated, each for perhaps five minutes. Occasionally a verse of a hymn broke the pattern after which a man and then a woman continued.

By the end of the hymn, the next speaker would be on her/his feet. One had to be both quick and aggressive to get a turn to speak. Hour after hour a shortage of preachers never occurred. The eloquence and confidence with which women spoke amazed me in light of the fact that on few other times in the year did they speak to an audience beyond their women's organization.

In 1988, Archbishop Motswaosele asked whether women should be ordained as ministers in the Spiritual Healing Church. I do not know his reasons for this step. It may simply have been his knowledge of the many capable women in the church. Women friends assured me that the women themselves had not raised the question; neither had they agitated for this step.

After much discussion, a decision followed at the national conference in August 1990. Women would be ordained to be preachers but not evangelists or full ministers (*baruti*). I heard that all of the women, plus some men, opposed the ordination of women as *baruti*. This possibility made women feel uncomfortable and confused. For them, the openness came "too early"; it might cause division within the church.

Early in 1991 Archbishop Motswaosele visited the Gaborone congregation to announce that the church constitution had been amended to allow women to be preachers. He then called two women to the pulpit to preach. Each spoke for about five minutes.

Motswaosele then pointed out that we had just observed women's ability to preach. This pragmatic method of deciding whether women should preach--"are they able to preach?"--intrigued me. Following this evidence, Motswaosele called for all women who wished to preach to come forward. Approximately thirty young women did so. The Archbishop then prayed for each one individually, that she might receive the gift of preaching.

I hope that the wisdom and insight which appears to guide decisions about gender roles, leadership, family life, and many other aspects of church life will continue to guide the Spiritual Healing Church.

6

"[S]he who plants a tree plants a hope."
Lucy Larcom

Five Hundred Years of Tears and Struggle

Elizabeth Soto Albrecht and Patricia Zapata

Women--the Hope for Latin America Today

Latin American woman--
Five hundred years giving birth to life
Five hundred years mourning the death of her children
assassinated, tortured, disappeared...
Five hundred years of hunger, poverty, violence, pain and rage...
Five hundred years of survival.

Latin American woman--
forger of dreams, happiness, love, creativity,
strength, dedication, commitment and identity.
Woman who waits and struggles for the hope of her own people.

Latin American woman-
giver and preserver of life and beliefs,
inspirer of faith; builder of roads for struggle,
alternative resistance, solidarity, peace.

Five hundred years after the invasion...
Woman means hope in Latin America.   --Patricia Zapata

Introduction - by Elizabeth Soto Albrecht
What can be said that historians and theologians have not already said to commemorate the arrival of Christopher Columbus to the New World? In order to seek truth, many people have reflected on the meaning of the

occasion. However, few women have given their opinion. Perhaps this is one more indicator of how history has been controlled by men. Women of Latin America have much to offer to the story of surviving, of keeping the culture alive by resisting the five-hundred-year-old conquest.

Aboriginal women have witnessed the transmogrification suffered by their culture since the arrival of the Spaniards to their lands. Rape, kidnapping, and death have been part of women's experience. Another misfortune that resulted directly from the invasion was the emergence of a macho attitude. The *mesizo* (a male born of an Indian woman and a Spaniard) tried to imitate the superiority complex of the conqueror. Rejected by both ethnic groups, such a male asserted power and control over his wife or mistress.

In November 1991, I addressed this subject at the Seminary of the Mennonite Church in Colombia. Teaching a course titled "Woman: Her Ministry, Identity and Hope for Latin America" proved to be one of my greatest experiences. It allowed women to express their feelings about these issues. It provided mutual learning as we reflected on scripture together, eager to find truth hidden from us for centuries.

Our mutual trust and hunger for truth uncovered women's roles in indigenous and peasant resistance. For example, we read a poem by Gioconda Belli of Nicaragua. This tells the women's story of Teguzgalpa (Tegucigalpa, current capital of Honduras). They refused to have intercourse with their warrior husbands because they feared their children would become slaves of the Spaniards. Belli's novel *La mujer habitada* tells the legend of indigenous people as written by Lopez de Gomara. She ends:

> That night we cried, embracing each other, resisting the desire of our bodies, surrounded by a deep sadness. We denied our lives, the prolongation, the germination of the seed...No woman of this tribe wants to give children for the construction of boats, for their bodies to be torn apart by dogs...

Belli reminds us that Latin American women continue to weep and struggle, but that they do so with hope.

How do they do this? Patricia Zapata, a journalist from Colombia, shares her journey with indigenous women in her country. Their struggles became hers. Her story sheds light on experiences of both conversion and hope. Hear what the community in San Jacinto offered to Patricia. (The privilege has been mine to translate her written work.)

THE WOMEN OF SAN JACINTO - by Patricia Zapata

I am not inspired by valleys, mountains, or beautiful landscapes, nor by theologians or political ideologies. I am inspired by life, by struggle, by everyday things. Like courage. Or the memory of faces of women I knew more than a decade ago. These were women in a Caribbean coastal town of Colombia, my country, plus women of the countryside. They were artisans and women of the *cumbia* dance, the hammock, and the machete--women of San Jacinto.

In this little town, as in hundreds throughout Latin America, women coexist. Daily survival is their common goal. Happiness, pain, poverty, death, hope, and resistance all coexist.

What will women commemorate in a five hundredth anniversary of an invasion--a totally hostile situation, a context of violence, social injustice, and the absence of human rights? We celebrate that we have more than the capacity to give and sustain life; women have more than a uterus. Even when exploited, marginalized, and oppressed, Latin American women have survived. In the midst of poverty, government violence, and family abuse, we have continued to build and to pursue alternatives.

We mothers, wives daughters, and widows focus on the survival of our children and families. We transform tears and pain into joy as we keep hope alive amidst need. Through hope, millions of women on this continent shape history. An unspoken resistance--peaceful and silent--gets written into the blood of our children. This holds true for women in San Jacinto and all of Colombia.

People live in miserable conditions of poverty; they lack social assistance. Their rustic houses, made of sticks and palm branches, comprise one room plus an open space without walls. The latter serves as a kitchen; three stones form a stove on the ground. Few houses have latrines for the six to eight people living there.

People lack public services--water and medical. Temperatures rise to forty degrees Celsius (104 Fahrenheit). Women and children store rain water in the rainy season. But during the dry season, they spend a great deal of time hauling it from cisterns or lagoons on the edge of town. The lack of potable water causes serious health problems, especially for children--enteritis, typhoid, cholera, and diarrhea being the most common.

Victims of poverty and violence wear a female face. Abandoned with five to seven children, a large percentage of women of San Jacinto receive very poor medical care or none at all. As a result of poverty, disease combined with malnutrition can be lethal. Women observe their children die, neglected by the government.

Militarism also functions like a cancer. Seemingly present only to militarize rural areas, the government offends impoverished people. Through repression and political persecution, many women in San Jacinto and Colombia become widows. Left empty-handed, they wonder what to do. Worst of all, after a husband's death, the women, their children, and organizations suffer similar persecution. However, in the midst of need and suffering, organizations take root. These bring people together, shoulder to shoulder. They take on great struggles, speak out, and seek alternatives. They demand and claim dignity and justice for people of San Jacinto, Colombia, and Latin America.

For five hundred years our people suffered, wept, and resisted injustice. While some acted through armed struggle, many women and children worked through peaceful, active resistance.

Some years ago, five of us women in San Jacinto were looking for an alternative to the daily grind of survival. Widowed and orphaned by violence, we met for a time of reflection. We voiced our anguish and fear. We sought ways to avoid the daily political persecution against our husbands, sons, fathers, and companions who were active in rural organizations. Thus was born the Women's Committee of San Jacinto.

Tasks multiplied. My lawyer husband had begun as an advisor to peasant groups. Working with conflict mediation and human rights issues, he helped peasants face the henchmen of the system. I had already been working on issues of identity and women's rights. Other women enriched the group: as wives of peasant leaders, one as the widow of a principle guerrilla leader.

Daily life became permanent warfare. Pitched battles and crossfire raged between military groups--government, guerrillas, paramilitary, self-defense groups, and drug traffickers. The unarmed, rural, civilian population struggled in the middle, attacked by whatever group thought its personal interest justified the action. San Jacinto stood in the middle of the war zone. Guerrilla takeovers of villages seemed likely; militarization of government forces seemed imminent.

Other actions followed. Members of the peasant organization were taken away at dawn, in front of their wives and children. Bodies of dead young men turned up in the streets. Our little children were harassed by soldiers--called "guerrilla brats"--frightened by weapons, and interrogated.

Violence against Committee families became constant and indiscriminate. Our group grew to twenty-six members. Many women came to the Committee to disclose their problems: serious domestic violence, rape, abandonment, beating, and slavery. The sale of daughters to well-to-do men of the area, called *dote* ("DOH-tay"), continues.

Because domestic and political violence had worsened, we decided to hold a silent march. Our first public demonstration urged respect for life and countered violence in the home and nation. Men, women, and children of the entire region participated.

Reflection and meetings continued. Out of them emerged the idea of cooperative farming. Facing great economic need, we began by raising eggplants, tomatoes, and corn. Resources for planting came from selling pastries and holding raffles. With farm products in hand, we began a small-scale cycle of self-financing. The organization kept itself together, focused around these activities and the initial problem of violence.

A long process followed. In time, we gathered strength to combat fear triggered by this work. While military and government intelligence agencies operated in the town, various groups of guerrillas infiltrated the countryside. In order to visit our Committees in more distant settlements, we had to pass through the territory of one or more groups. They interrogated us. Personal struggles and chores also continued at home. Several of us had babies.

We made long journeys on foot, carrying babies. Hungry and thirsty, we went to meetings during rain or bright sun. We helped women who were burdened with children and chores. We spoke of human rights and women's rights, of needs and violence that assailed us.

For example, some husbands beat their wives almost to death. At times, other husbands among us helped us intervene. In a peaceful way, we confronted wife beaters. With their behavior exposed to neighbors, friends, and companions, they became less violent. Exceptions appeared. Encounters as advocates also prompted us to look at relationships in our own homes.

As a result of cooperative effort, the group gained respect and credibility. It provided a safe space for expressing deep-felt needs and for seeking alternatives. This led us to consult other organizations. We sought direct help for dealing with problems of health, water, and injustice. As we claimed our rights and pursued more productive projects, we became much better known.

But political violence increased too. Organizational growth brought with it exposure. State security forces made us the target of their power and destruction. All kinds of aggression followed--threats, torture at every level, persecution, break-ins, continuous arrests. A force of eighty armed men--soldiers and police combined--broke into my house. They aimed their weapons at me and my four children who were then seven and eight years and six and eighteen months old. They threw everything around and stole several items. They had already detained my husband, along with fifteen husbands of Women's Committee members.

Our work became paralyzed for a while, due to fear. However, a new dynamic emerged. Of some principles we were sure. We had to continue the cooperative production efforts. We had to resist. We could not allow our work to be declared subversive or illegal. Our programs allowed us to work and earn modest income for our children and ourselves. When the military questioned us, we named our cooperative work as an excuse for meeting. Doing that, cohesion returned. We understood that we had to struggle as a group.

Our meetings knew tears, rage, and finally proposals of hope. We had to train ourselves, breaking bonds with other groups of women around the country. An interesting feature of the process arose in San Jacinto. Although several of the women were then, or had earlier been, companions of guerrillas, none of them chose violence or weapons. On the contrary, they chose an alternative. The daily struggle--notable because of our organization's one hundred children--led us to discuss and act on non-violent options.

More than a thousand kilometers now separate me from San Jacinto. But I cannot forget all my friends and companions in the struggle: the black women of Palenque, the people of other towns, those we met while bonding to seek identity and reach out.

Life shared with Ana, Melida, Rocio, Brigida, Silvia and so many others proved to be rich. These women taught me solidarity, togetherness, and affection. They taught me the courage of the land, the wealth of its folklore, the *cumbia* dance, the people's dreams. Together we found the strength to confront silence--the painful admission of powerlessness. With them, I learned to listen with the uterus. With them, I became converted into my own self. One is not born a woman; one has to become a woman, to assume the identity, to have birthed the life force. For, woman is life.

Our challenge as Latin American women continues to foster that kind of culture. To identify with type, class, and faith. To resist being extinguished by poverty, repression or violence. The story of the women of San Jacinto does not stand alone; many on our continent wait to be told.

Several years ago, my family and I had to flee the town, as did others. At that time the Committee had thirty members. Within three years it grew to one hundred ninety-six. They became an Association with fifteen neighborhood committees. These offered various training programs in the Center where we used to live. With representation, they made decisions in national peasant organizations. They had a workshop and storage area for making clothes and crafts. In the Center several members taught for the community school. Most of the students came from families of widows and persecuted people.

Women of San Jacinto retain their hope for tomorrow. Hope expresses their greatest act of faith. For them, faith has a life-long dimension. It includes resistance and struggle. It confronts social and class realities. Although political violence has not ceased to sow pain and more poverty, many groups of Latin American women continue to confront the hazards.

This story testifies to and extends praise for women. Precisely because of this account, we must recognize ourselves. After five hundred years of invasion and resistance, women have followed a distinct process, whether history mentions it or not. Silent and slowly, it will continue through ingredients of survival, resistance, and pacifist alternatives.

With confidence I declare: in violent Latin America, a gestation occurs of fundamental changes that will form new generations to defend the children of the majority. Such a counter-culture of active non-violence reflects the nature and origin of women's organizations. It produces changes and carries imbedded a silent revolution. It affects the autocratic and violent practices of our society. It informs the history of our peoples and nations. *Women equal Hope for Latin America.*

7 *"I rest me in the thought of rocks and trees..."*
Maltbie D. Babcock

Stories from South Africa

Judy Zimmerman Herr

"I Chose God"

Her large size only outwardly indicates her strength and stability. Prophetess Manyadu, founder and leader of the St. Paul's Faith mission of Transkei, proves to be strong of spirit as well. Her home and church in Ngangalizwe, the old "location" (black housing area) of Umtata, is a refuge of peace and healing for those who come seeking help. Here they grow strong on good food, rest, prayer, and the laying-on of hands.

Her story does not begin here. For many years she worked as a maid in a white suburb of Johannesburg.

"I raised their little boy," she says, "and now he is a grown man." But she has never heard from him.

"These whites, they don't keep your friendship when they are finished with you." She shakes her head sadly.

In Johannesburg she became more and more involved in the church where her gifts of prayer and healing became apparent. Then, one day, she faced a serious choice.

"I was praying in my room with some others, and I forgot that the dinner was cooking. My master smelled the meat burning; he came out to my room, very angry. He told me that I must choose between my church or my job."

At first she was frightened and said she wanted her job, but after a while her troubled conscience won out, and she quit the job and moved to the black "homeland" area of the Transkei where her family originally lived.

"I chose God," she says, "and I have not been sorry."

She did not intend to found a church. For a time, she lived as a "prayer woman." People would come to her house for prayers and healing, and gradually a church took root. The work has not always been easy. She still tries to convince the authorities to grant to her the land on which to build a church--the house they meet in currently fails to be large enough.

But her authority and her gifts are not questioned. She is also a leader among the group of independent churches located in Ngangalizwe. Perhaps because of their greater emphasis on spiritual gifts, the independent churches are much less reluctant than the mission churches to allow women positions of leadership.

"Denying women a role," says one of the Zionist bishops emphatically, "is just not biblical!"

Prophetess Manyadu's church, with its uniforms and all-night services, its clapping and dancing, differs considerably from what I have known. Yet, I can readily identify with her as a sister in faith. I can look up to her as one who followed God and used her gifts, even though she did not know where that would take her.

Wearing a Black Sash

They have been looked down on at times by members of radical black organizations struggling for justice in South Africa. True, they are mostly wealthy, white, privileged--"the wives of the oppressors." And yet, for over fifty years they have been there, standing silently along the roads and in front of the government buildings, wearing their black sashes.

The Black Sash, a women's organization, was formed in the late 1940's in South Africa. The Afrikaner Nationalist Party had just come into power on the platform of apartheid--complete separation of the races. One of its first moves brought change to the constitution. It removed the "Coloured" (mixed race) population from the voter rolls in the Cape Province. They were the only non-white South Africans who had the right to vote. Angered at this disregard for the rule of law, a group of white, middle-class women donned black sashes and marched through the streets of Cape Town. With that symbol, they mourned the loss of constitutionality.

In the years that followed, laws in South Africa became more restrictive. Marches and demonstrations were for many years illegal. The women of the Black Sash continued to protest, standing silently just far enough apart in order not to constitute a "group." They have protested the imposition of laws that determined a person's area of work, living, education, and burial on the basis of race. They have stood against detentions without trial and the death penalty. They have been at the forefront of documenting forced removals of communities discredited because of the "wrong" race.

Along with their protests, the Black Sash women have operated offices from which to share advice. These have helped workers sort their way through the maze of paperwork which apartheid regulations demand--passes, job permits, pensions. They have published regular reports analyzing government action on labor laws and land use regulations.

Sheena Duncan personifies the Black Sash for many in South Africa. Sheena's mother was a founding member of the organization. She herself has served as national president and as head of the network of advice offices. A committed Christian, Sheena also serves as a vice president of the South African Council of Churches and as a member of a national Human Rights Monitoring Group.

Sheena acknowledges the Black Sash as an organization of the privileged and powerful. "There was self-interest involved, at the beginning, among the predominate English-speaking white women who started the group."

They feared the Afrikaner government. Those were the people who had been defeated by the British in a bloody war thirty years before. Now they might use their power to do away with rights of the English South Africans as well as the blacks. But the organization has grown since then in its understanding and awareness of justice issues.

"The advice offices really helped us, because they made us aware of how apartheid affected the majority of the people," Sheena says.

Now one of many organizations in South Africa to work for justice and the rule of law, the Black Sash previously stood almost alone.

"When we moved back to South Africa after some time away in 1964," says Sheena, "I joined the Black Sash because that's all there was. Now there are so many groups working against apartheid, but that wasn't the case then." Through all these years, the women with their black sashes have stood in silent but clear testimony. They will continue to stand against all human rights violations.

"The Bleeding Heart of Jesus"

I met Sister Camilla at a workshop on active nonviolent strategy in 1988. The workshop, held in Lesotho, a tiny country surrounded by South Africa, gathered together South African church workers. They had come to explore ways in which churches could be more intentional about their actions in response to apartheid repression.

The workshop began with an exercise, getting to know one another. At the front of the room stood a large drawing of a human body. We were asked to identify ourselves as one part of the body, which symbolized the Body of Christ. What particular function in the Body did we represent? After time to reflect, we each chose a partner with whom to share our thoughts. My partner was Sister Camilla.

"I think," she said, "that I am the bleeding heart of Jesus--bleeding because it feels and carries all the pain of the world."

Surrounded by people who chose to identify themselves as feet, hands, ears, eyes--functional, active parts--Camilla went right to the center, the part which feels and bears the pain.

As I came to know her better over the next few days, I saw how right she had been, to describe herself like that. A contemplative Anglican religious who lives as part of a community in the mountains of Lesotho, Camilla defines her work as prayer--and it's hard work. Camilla usually doesn't attend workshops, but she was given permission to come to this one because her community sensed the crucial issue. Her presence there served as a constant reminder that among the forms of nonviolent, direct action that Christians might engage in against injustice, prayer ranks high.

Camilla did not grow up aspiring to be a contemplative. In fact, she says that her becoming one must have been from God. It seemed far removed from or beyond her personal self-image. Rather, she was an activist, involved in political struggles for change in her community in Cape Town.

Her family had suffered forced removals. After their home in Cape Town was destroyed, they moved into an area for "Coloureds," away from the center of "white" Cape Town. Growing up in this setting, she endured politicization early, from school days.

But in the midst of her activism, she says, a void or emptiness surfaced. When her pastor suggested that she might become a sister, she expressed shock. "That's not me!" she thought. And yet the inner nudging persisted. Becoming a contemplative, in the end, became her way of being active for God.

A life of prayer is not easy, not to be taken on lightly, Camilla says. Convinced of its importance within God's work, Camilla and the others in her community remain in touch with a large network of people in South Africa and elsewhere in the world through prayer. They often receive invitations from church leaders in South Africa to be in prayer during meetings, conferences, and demonstrations.

After the workshop, I visited briefly with Camilla in her community. Seemingly an island of peace and quiet, nestled among the hills, it also provides extensive action. Both withdrawn and connected, it holds and feels the pain of the world. There, Camilla and others work to express through prayer "the bleeding heart of Jesus."

DETERMINED

Lisa Schirch

your power is not tied
to these sitcom life-echoing episodes

i sit amazed and awesome-eyed
at your Self and Land

Self-discovery birthing self-understanding
into self power...
Self determined

the dis-ease of apathy
foreboding on every tv screen
warning of land never hand-touched
nor heart-touched

those sacred, earth-tied blessings...
connectedness unknown
to me and my race

Leading the Way: First Nations Women in Canada
"Women are the core of our communities." "Women's power is strong, spiritual power." I have heard these words often in Native communities or when listening to traditional First Nation elders. The women I have encountered in the past decade bring this wisdom to life.

Sarah, an Innu elder, continues to live most of the year in the bush. While she speaks a bit of English, her first language is Innuamuin. She struggles to pass on Innu culture and language to her children. She also struggles to stop NATO from practicing low-level flying over lands her people have occupied for the past nine thousand years. She has feared for her family's safety as jets create sonic booms by flying just over the treetops near people's tents. She has also led her family onto the runways at the Goose Bay Military Base. She has spent six months in jail--a high price for seeking justice.

Eva, an Ojibway woman, grew up on Manitoulin Island. She remembers her parents' teachings well. They warned her that Mother Earth was being poisoned. She remembers the pain of being forcibly removed from her parents by an "Indian agent" who took her to the residential school run by Catholic nuns. She wonders why the *shoognosh* (white people) want to ruin both Mother Earth and the *Nishnawbe* (Native people).

Dana, a Metis woman, knows very little about her Native roots. While her mother is an Ojibway, she lost her Indian status by marrying a non-Native. Her mother was ashamed of her "Nativeness"; she considered it a fault or something to be covered up. Now Dana searches out her roots. She is determined to become an "Indian," both legally and culturally.

As a non-Native woman working as Native Concerns Coordinator for Mennonite Central Committee, I felt honored to meet and become friends with many Native women. Three women[1] taught me a great deal about power and the need for self-determination. While Native women remain part of the larger First Nations' movement to have their right to self-determination acknowledged, the leadership and integrity Native women bring to the struggle form important contributions. As a non-Native, I see the struggle of Native women through my own cultural lenses. Since I cannot speak for Native women, I will describe here what I have learned from them.

The First Nations' Struggle for Self-Determination
The year 1992 marked the five-hundredth anniversary of Columbus' arrival in the Americas. Aboriginal groups throughout the hemisphere marked the year in special ways. Some mourned what has been lost. Others celebrated their survival. One of the more significant movements emphasized "self-discovery."

The "Self-Discovery Campaign" addresses everyone who has suffered under colonialism. In particular, it strives to strengthen the cultural identity and self-determination of Aboriginal peoples.[2] The First Nations of Canada provide an example of the self-discovery movement. Out of a history of oppression and injustice, they provide a model for creating justice or "right relations" for all people.

The history of the First Nations gives witness to the paternal attitudes that have created the current dynamics. While the French and British treated the First Nations as valued trading partners and as allies in successive wars for the first three hundred years of colonization, their cooperation with the First Nations gave way to a coercive relationship as the colonizing nations established themselves.[3]

The First Nations were soon treated as an obstacle to the progress of the Europeans. Treaties lay broken and land stolen, while the Federal government enacted laws to control every movement of the First Nations.[4] Laws outlawed Native rituals and forcibly removed children from their parents to be put into schools where they were punished for speaking their language or practicing their culture. Until the last fifty-plus years, the First Nations could not vote or hire a lawyer to protect their rights and treaties. Many of the oppressive laws that governed the First Nations have only recently been repealed.[5] Years of unjust treatment by a society trying to melt the First Nations into their own mold have created dependence and antagonism.

This legacy of colonialism has not quelled the First Nations' desire to regain self-determination and form a just relationship with the rest of Canada. By first rediscovering their culture, they have found the source of their power. Unique aspects of their culture, such as its relational and environmental orientation, stand at the root of much of their struggle. Respect for the earth and everything on it is of utmost importance. While at one time, some Natives felt ashamed of their culture and identity, today Native culture experiences increased respect and admiration.

The First Nations want to work with the rest of Canada to form a society authentically inclusive, relational, and respectful of all distinct societies.[6] In recent years, the diverse aspirations of Native people for self-determination have been voiced in the term "self-government." The First Nations want to be treated as a "people," not simply as a numerical "population."[7] They want to set up their own schools and have their children taught in their native languages. They want to secure a land base and gain more control over resource development projects on their land. They want to use indigenous governing systems that were in place long before colonizers introduced new political and legal systems. While self-government could take as many forms as there are nations or communities, the term has emerged as the most effective way the First Nations can communicate their vision of a future within Canada.

First Nation Women

In particular, First Nation women are leading their communities to regain power to control their lives.[8] Many Native cultures are matrilineal and highly respectful of women's gifts. When Europeans first arrived in North America, Native women had great economic, political and legal power. While First Nation men and women had prescribed roles, neither sex claimed less or more importance. As Europeans tightened their control of the "new world," the First Nations' matriarchal and egalitarian societies knew severe damage. The newcomers "insisted on dealing only with First Nation men," and, while First nation women usually controlled the property of the tribe, "dealings with women were minimized and gradually eliminated."[9]

Today, Native women struggle against centuries of oppression. Before 1982's *Canadian Charter of Rights and Freedoms* came into effect, Native women experienced severe discrimination under the *Indian Act,* which since 1876 has governed every aspect of a Native person's life. The *Indian Act* ensured that Indian women who married non-Indian men lost their Indian status.[10] Indian men who married non-Indian women did not lose their status; instead, their non-Indian wives *gained* Indian status. While this legal identity struggle was eventually won, the process for reinstating "status" for Native women who had previously lost it has been extremely slow.

Unfortunately, many Native women find that they must not only struggle against the federal government's *Indian Act*, but against the Aboriginal male establishment created under the *Indian Act.* In fact, the most well-known First Nations' political organization, the Assembly of First Nations, opposed the repeal of laws that limit status for Indian women.[11]

More recently, the Native Women's Association of Canada (NWAC) has tried to persuade both the Canadian government and First Nation political organizations that they should be included in the discussion of entrenching the right to self-government in the Canadian constitution. In a press release, NWAC explained their right as women to have a voice in deciding upon the definition of Aboriginal government powers.

> It is not simply a case of recognizing that we have a right to self-determination and self-government. Aboriginal women also have sexual equality rights. We want those rights respected. Governments cannot simply choose to recognize the patriarchal forms of government which now exist in our communities. The

band councils and the Chiefs who preside over our lives
are not our traditional forms of government...We want
community decision making.[12]

In essence, NWAC strives to assure the individual rights of
women while Aboriginal governments seek to secure their collective
rights of sovereignty.

Many traditional First Nations' women and men strive to
reinstate the traditional forms of government and to again place women
at the core of their communities. They call for self-government based
on "equality and fairness, consultation and peaceful dialogue, respect for
diversity, compassion and generosity" by strengthening the voice and
participation of Aboriginal women whose priorities include their
families. By emphasizing women's contribution to self-government,
First Nation communities can regain the strength and spiritual power
they once held.[13]

In some First Nation communities, women already exercise their
right to self-determination and to regain their place of leadership to heal
and strengthen their communities. In Nitassinan (Labrador), Innu
women lead their community's resistance to the military's exploitation of
their land. In many northern Ontario communities, Native women lead
the struggle against domestic violence and addiction. In the community
of Attawapiskat, Native women elders help decide how offenders should
be punished by the justice system. At the Six Nations reserve, where the
traditional Iroquois constitution is still used, clan mothers choose the
chief of the community.

Conclusion

Despite centuries of paternalism and pressure to assimilate, both
First Nations' women and men still struggle to hold onto their identity.
First Nations' women in particular have much to offer their own
societies by regaining their traditional positions of power. By rooting
their struggle in the ongoing process of self-discovery and by
recognizing and acting upon the right to determine their lives, the First
Nations gain not only the attention and respect of more and more
Canadians. They provide models for how non-Natives and our own
governments can gain relational, inclusive and respectful aspects for our
own lives.

Endnotes
   1. Names have been changed.

2. Paul McKenna. "1992--Theology of Self-Discovery Offers Hope," *Catholic New Times*, March 1990, p. 4.

3. James R. Miller. *Skyscrapers Hide the Heavens*, Toronto:University of Toronto Pr, 1989.

4. Boyce Richardson, ed. *Drum Beat*, Toronto:Summerhill Pr, 1989.

5. Geoffrey York. *The Dispossessed: Life and Death in Native Canada*, London:Vintage U.K., 1990.

6. Murray Angus. *...And the Last Shall be First: Native Policy in an Era of Cutbacks*, Toronto:NC Pr, 1991.

7. Julian Burger. *The Gaia Atlas of First Peoples*, Toronto:Anchor Books, 1990.

8. Julie Fels. "What do Native Women Want?" *Everywoman's Almanac 1992*, Toronto:Women's Pr, 1991.

9. Native Women's Association of Canada. *Matriarchy and the Canadian Charter*, Ottawa, 1992, p. 5.

10. "Status Indians" are entitled to a number of special privileges that are not given to "non-status Indians."

11. Native Women's Association of Canada. *Statement on the Canada Package*, Ottawa, 1992, p. 3.

12. *Ibid.*, p. 8.

13. NWAC. *Matriarchy...*, p. 7.

9

"...as in the cone the tree."
Daniel Webster Whittle

Fitting Some Pieces Together: Lives of Vietnamese Women

Janet Umble Reedy

The Wife

Granite boulder, astride the mountain peak
Silently surveys the harbor.
The people see a woman waiting for a ship
    to bring her husband home.

One day, with muddy feet and aching back,
She climbed the mountain.
One thousand years of planting rice and carrying it to market
    lay behind her,
In front of her, anticipation,
At last, rewarded only by the empty blue horizon.

Her hungry children cry alone,
But she, in stone, waits here forever.

Note: Along the coast in central Vietnam there is a large rock which, with imagination, can be seen as a woman looking toward the horizon. The villagers call this formation, "Woman Waiting for her Husband."

The cultivation of rice in a tropical country with capricious weather conditions--storms, floods and droughts--is a labour-consuming and strenuous work. Immense expanses of fields and the silhouettes of Vietnamese peasant women, bent under the scorching sun transplanting rice or leg-deep in cold mud irrigating their paddy fields in winter, have been associated with each other for thousands of years...

Women of the aristocracy, educated in the...traditions of devotion and courage, took charge of the family in the absence of the 'great pillar of the household'--their husbands...

As for women of the common people, they had to work with their husbands to feed their children. But as their husbands were often conscripted into the army, or for corvees or public works, they had to struggle alone.

From: Mai Thi Tu and Le Thi Nham Tuyet. *Women in Vietnam*, Hanoi:Foreign Languages Publishing House, 1978, 63-4, 68.

The Mother

The child's incessant wail
Destroys the silence of the sleeping village.

The neighbors stir,
Complaining that they cannot sleep.
Yet, with good-natured sympathy, forgive,
"She cries because her mother has no milk."

The mother contemplates the child beside her in the darkness
She who has survived drought and falling bombs,
Has eaten sweet potatoes when the rice is gone,
Knows that her daughter cries the tears she cannot shed.

Wrestling with the darkness, the oil lamp's quivering flame
Illuminates the future,
Exposing with stark clarity the harsh life bequeathed by mother
        to her daughter.
But powerless to overcome the shadows of the poor room
        in which they lie.

She does not hush the crying child.

The Widow

"How has the celebration of the New Year changed since you were a girl?" we asked the grandmother.

"It hasn't changed at all. It is just the same," she replied. She said this as she shared with us the same special dishes of chicken, pork, sticky rice cake, and bamboo shoots that she had eaten to celebrate most of the eighty New Year's festivals of her life.

We are sitting, together with some of her children and grandchildren, in her room. The room has a shabby elegance. Like most homes in Hanoi, it has not been painted for many years. But it is furnished with a carved antique bed and cupboard inlaid with mother-of-pearl. In the cupboard are antique porcelain bowls and vases. The hard wooden bed is covered with the woven straw mat on which the grandmother sleeps. The traditional "Tet bush," a small pink flowering peach tree, adds color to the room for the New Year's celebration.

She is a stately woman, gray hair pulled back from her face in a bun. She wears the clothes of old women--black silk, wide-bottomed pants and a long-sleeved over-blouse, fitted at the bust, with buttons down the front.

She was the oldest child in her family. "I wasn't allowed to have a real education," she explained. "My education was to learn to fulfill my responsibilities as a daughter and wife and mother according to the Vietnamese feudal family system."

She married when she was 22. Within ten years she had six children. Then her husband, an army officer, was killed. That was nearly fifty years ago. In this house where she still lives, she raised her six children by herself. She has just shown us a picture of herself, a widow of 35 dressed in a traditional embroidered Vietnamese long tunic over her wide-bottomed pants, with her six smiling children--three daughters and three sons.

We know some of these children. Two live in France (where one has married a French woman and is criticized by the family for raising his three sons like Frenchmen who do not speak Vietnamese.) Her youngest son, born shortly before her husband's death, tragically died several years ago. "She loved him the most," says the oldest daughter, and no one disagrees.

The others, with their children and grandchildren, still live in this house with her. She made sure that her sons and her daughters had a real education. She is proud that they, and their spouses and their children, are doctors, teachers, engineers, journalists, pharmacists, and artists. She considers their accomplishment to be in part hers. As some of them listen to her tell the story again, I detect that they have heard it many times.

"I had many offers of marriage..."

"She was very beautiful," her daughter-in-law interrupts.

"But according to the feudal values which I was taught, I should not re-marry. So I didn't. I raised my children alone and remained poor. If I had it to do over again, I would remarry."

She speaks in the presence of her recently widowed 39-year-old daughter-in-law. The daughter-in-law and her two young daughters live in a small house connected to the large house. In the small three-room house, one room is reserved for the altar. There, they make offerings of fruit and flowers. They burn candles and incense every day in memory of the beloved youngest son, husband, father, and brother. His portrait dominates the room.

The daughter-in-law wears a black armband in mourning. She cries when she talks about her husband; she has taken a year's leave from her teaching job in order to grieve. This New Year, tradition dictates that she must not pay a visit to another home for fear she will pass on her own bad luck. She worries about her daughters' education and their future. For now, her days appear to revolve around family obligation.

But her mother-in-law's advice is clear. "Don't live your life as I've lived mine!"

The role and status of Vietnamese women has changed dramatically in the last 50-100 years from appalling subordination and exploitation of women during the colonial, feudal and Chinese eras. During the war women were able to prove themselves as capable and equal to men and, as a result, the constitution and subsequent legislation of the new independent state is impressive in its clear and emphatic statements on the rights and role of women. Also, compared to most other Asian societies, women in Vietnam are particularly independent and their position supported and protected by progressive legislation. However, there are signs that since re-unification and peace, the position of women is slipping back, with a steady decrease in the representation of women in political life and positions of responsibility, reappearance of some traditional attitudes and practices, inequality of opportunity and workload. However, in spite of a certain residual tendency to undervalue themselves, there is also a strong streak of pugnaciousness and independence in Vietnamese women which helps to undermine this tendency.

From: Susan Allen. "Women in Vietnam," Report Commissioned by the Swedish International Development Authority, Appendix 4, p. 14, Hanoi, May 1990.

_____

The Farmer

A short woman with black, wavy hair, she dresses in the style of a Vietnamese professional woman--dark slacks, pumps, a stylish blouse with soft lines. She smiles often. But her manner is businesslike, giving the impression of a person who has important decisions to make and serious problems to solve. In her fifties, she is the rector of one of Vietnam's leading agricultural universities and a member of the National Assembly.

When she was nine years old, her family moved from the city to the country. Her father, a doctor, had been assigned to work in a village so small that it had no school. So she went to live with a family in another village where she could attend school. She worked in the rice fields to pay for her room and board.

Then, as now, women did most of the fieldwork in Vietnam. She saw them barefoot in the irrigated fields, bending over to plant each seedling one by one. They pulled weeds, harvested the stalks with a knife when the grain was ripe, beat the harvested rice to separate the grain from the stalks, spread it in the sun to dry, and carried it in baskets suspended from a pole which rested on their shoulders.

"As I watched them and worked with them, I understood how hard the farm women's lives are."

When she finished high school, she decided to study agriculture.

"I wanted to learn how to make the lives of the farmers easier, so I went into farm machinery engineering. I thought that there must be a way to make machines do some of the work."

She was one of two women who passed the examinations for entrance into the agricultural university in her class. A student practicum took her back to the rice fields. But this time she was driving a tractor.

"We ploughed day and night and the village people came to watch us. It was the first time that many of them had seen tractors. They were amazed to see the machines doing the work they had always done with only the strength of their bodies."

She was an outstanding student. When graduated, she was asked to stay at the university as an instructor. Traditionally, many Vietnamese students go abroad to study. After a few years, she began to study Chinese to prepare herself for graduate study in China. However, the onset of the Cultural Revolution interrupted those plans. She shifted her study to Russian and was selected to go to the Soviet Union for graduate study. She observed that the lives of the people were much easier there.

"Compared with Vietnam, life in the Soviet Union at that time was a paradise!"

Farmers had machines to do much of their work. She determined to adapt what she had learned to the conditions in Vietnam.

When she returned, she was appointed dean of the faculty of farm machinery engineering. This was during the war years and the Americans were dropping bombs on the city of Hanoi. Once again, as in her childhood, she moved to the country. This time, the entire university faculty and student body moved from the outskirts of the city to the country to get out of bombing range. Because of the war emergency, students and faculty combined farm work with their academic work, helping the local farmers to produce food for the nation.

Within a few years the war was over and the university moved back to its suburban location. She was promoted to vice-rector and then rector of the university.

The first years as rector were extremely difficult. All the country's resources had gone into winning the war. The economy was a shambles. All sectors of society were in need of reconstruction and development. But the university, as well as the rest of the country, had few resources, other than the labor of the people, with which to rebuild.

She also met other obstacles.

"I had authority over men and many of them had been my teachers. They were men and they were older than I. In spite of my position, they still saw me as their inferior because I am a woman. By this time, I had married another professor in the university. When my colleagues could not deny that I was doing a good job, they said,

'She can do it because her husband tells her how!'

"So I persuaded him to go abroad to study for several years, to show that I could successfully administer the university even without him!

"I showed them, but I have always had to work very hard to stay ahead of my critics. It is important to get directly involved in the tasks of administration and teaching so that I really understand what is going on in the university. It is important always to be prepared for any challenge, and to know how to select which problem to tackle first. I try to anticipate every possible objection or problem that will result from any course of action, so that I am ready with a solution for everything.

"I was already in my thirties when I married. I persuaded my husband that my work was important, and he agreed that we should have only one child. My son is now a university student. It takes good organization of the household so that I can devote myself to my work. My husband has shown understanding. At first he was a little threatened by my position, but it's all right because at home he is the king!"

The memories of the young girl who planted and harvested rice keep her teaching and research connected to the real problems of the farmers in the villages. Broad-based reforms, which move Vietnam from a collective economy to a market-based economy, are creating a need for changes in agricultural education. Now individual farmers must make management and marketing decisions that formerly were made for them by the leaders of their cooperatives. As in the past, women continue to do the majority of the farm work. The rector works together with the Vietnam Women's Union, at both the national and local levels, to improve services for women.

"We provide training and services that enable the farm women to carry out gardening and animal husbandry projects to increase the family income. But I am also concerned about other aspects of the lives of farm women. They must know about more than food production. They must also have a broad knowledge of society. I cannot forget the barefoot women in the rice paddies!"

Hanoi, Vietnam   May 1991

10

Diverse Voices from India

Dorothy Yoder Nyce

Part I. Aruna Gnanadason's Visionary Compassion

> Therefore, the search for a community of people where all will find space for creativity and fulfillment, a community that will live in real peace with justice, a community that will be ever alert to its responsibility to give birth to new life by challenging forces of death-- this is the most important characteristic of Asian women's spirituality.[1]

> What is unique about Christian theism is the unique mission that we have been given to share the liberating essence of the Gospel.[2]

> What we mean by feminist theology in India, and in fact the Third World, is theology from the perspective of women in struggle.[3]

[Note: The above statements from theologian Aruna Gnanadason appear in:

1 'Women and Spirituality in Asia," *Theology from the Third World A Reader*, Ursula King, ed., p. 353; also in *In God's Image*, Dec 1989.

2 "Living in Harmony with Each Other: A Feminist Perspective," Speech prepared for Mennonite Central Committee's 1994 Peace Theology Colloquium, printed in "Peace Theology in a Pluralistic World," *The Conrad Grebel Review*, Winter 1996, p. 97

3 "Towards an Indian Feminist Theology," *We Dare to Dream Doing Theology as Asian Women*, Virginia Fabella & Sun Ai Lee Park, eds., p. 117.]

Such vision and compassion permeate Gnanadason's writing and personal conversation. In fact, she intentionally combines writing from a desk with direct involvement in efforts for justice. As present coordinator of the Women's Programme and the World Council of Churches' Unit III/Justice, Peace, Creation, she writes to encourage, inform, and prod. She also is actively engaged, having traveled to several continents during the WCC's Ecumenical Decade of Churches in Solidarity with Women. From meeting hundreds of women, she values leaders and commoners alike, be they street children in Brazil or violated, brave women in South Africa.

When my daughter Lynda and I visited Aruna in Madras, India, 1990, she took us to the CDWS (Centre for Development and Women's Studies) before her own home. The Centre acts as legal advocate for urban, poor women. It helps women understand their rights and works in their behalf in court settings. Aruna told of how some women can be belittled by judges or the court system, when not accompanied by a defender.

The quantity of programs carried out from two rented flats (apartments) amazed me. A remarkable library collection--books, "cuttings," and notebooks on themes--awaits those able to read. Staff members find that the attention span of some women who visit the Centre lasts little more than ten minutes. Yet, those same women will skip a day of work/income and spend four rupees for bus fare to join Centre activities. During our visit, girls (grades 4-5) also enjoyed the safe, welcoming space in which to draw pictures.

A profound, dual task pervades Aruna's theology: to be in solidarity with people of all faiths through witness to common spiritual being, and to make authentic the covenant Jesus offers by standing with any "poor" and against all that destroys life. Whereas patriarchy--the system of oppression, graded subjugation, and hierarchical relationships--identifies those dominated as "other," the new feminist paradigm requires solidarity with all oppressed groups, Aruna believes.

Christian scriptures both liberate and destroy. Certain texts have driven some believers toward fundamentalist, triumphalist trends. They attempt to "keep women in their place"; they presume to exclude. But when women use their experience in the struggle for liberation as the point of departure for doing theology, they transform God's word of salvation--they live out the message of righting wrong. In such faith, Aruna speaks and lives.

Appropriately, Gnanadason examines spirituality through *Shakti* or *devi*, the energy underlying the cosmos and depicted through the Earth Mother. Prominent in India, and based on five thousand years of tradition, the Asian spiritual power of *Shakti* never totally yielded to the European, male-oriented system of knowledge that dominates western thought and practice. Rather than limit spirituality to personal prayer or asceticism, *all* of experience shapes the inner core. And Aruna understands the spirituality that then emerges from *Han*. Korean theologians describe *Han* as that sense which arises through exploited and powerless people when they express, name, and change from their sense of abandonment.

Aruna comprehends why many Asian women respond with a "hermeneutics of suspicion." Traditional spiritualities, interpretations of scriptures, and even analysis of society have often neglected the most oppressed. But through renewed *Shakti*, or spiritual energy, Asian feminists affirm the community dimension of Asian society. They critique a development model that pressures the poor to sustain the burden of "progress." They counter majority religions that call for uniformity and minority groups intent to preserve their identity at all costs. In celebration of plurality, they also draw strength from ancient popular religion that became a force for social justice. As women, or any oppressed people, transform pain into political power, they express deep spirituality. Their songs and stories affirm the liberator God; they envision a new world order, framed by compassion.

So, what prepared Aruna for doing theology on a global scale? Before joining the All India Council of Christian Women in 1982, Aruna worked as English lecturer and later as program secretary of the Ecumenical Christian Centre in Whitefield, Bangalore. She also served as a secretary in India's National Christian Council in the Unit on Witness and Service. Since then, she has been involved not only in the national scene but in various international programs. After being a vice-moderator, she became the Director of the Sub-unit on women in the World Council of Churches.

Aruna and I first met in a Madras hotel lobby, in June 1988. She inspired me. Aruna's vision and compassion appear in the following excerpts from our taped conversation:

"First, I'll tell you a little about the strong, very well organized, women's movement in India. It spreads all over the country--largely in the big cities but also with strength in rural areas...

"Although the All India Women's Conference has met annually since 1925, the movement knew a surge in the 1940s with the Telengana Peasant uprising--against oppression in British India. Energized, the women's movement followed the Independence movement.

"The impetus for the current phase of the movement began with the rape by two policemen of a fourteen-year-old girl Mathura, in 1978. Women organized; two from Delhi opened the case in India's Supreme Court...

"Women rediscovered earlier efforts by women--after the Freedom Struggle. International Women's Year and the Decade that followed gave more impetus. Now the movement extends considerably, addressing more than rape and oppression. Women realize that they must work at national issues. They have become serious in talking about feminism as an alternative, beginning now...

"In the case of communalism [ultra-loyal religious communities], the women's movement has brought us together--beyond class or caste or whatever. We need to become an anti-communalist force...

"Of course ecology has always been a big cause. We have a history of a lot of justice issues--water, trees, and affects of technology like genetics or amniocentesis [sex determination] tests. Trends show how actively women participate in all of these. For example, some women took a petition regarding the abuse of injected contraceptives to the Supreme Court. Many cooperate to mobilize public opinion. The whole question of peace and justice continues as active agenda for women throughout India, and Asia...

"We often connect with secular women's groups from other Asian countries. We join together on issues of prostitution and tourism, plus militarization. Two years ago in Thailand fifty women--three activists from each country--discussed militarization and its effects on women. Because of political division and ideological differences, we did not create a unified statement. But solid support and a network of relationships emerged through sharing information about our own countries...

"A strong sense of commonality is emerging through the discussion of feminist theology. Sun Ai Park, a strong leader, nudges all of us along. Chung Hyun Kyung is also fantastic, helping us to be rightfully proud to be Asian. In God's Image [an Asian women's journal] is a perfect example of Asian feminist hermeneutics. So grounded in justice questions, Asian women need to say more clearly what feminism means for us and what its contribution can be..."

[My personal journal entry reflects on this taped conversation.]
"I feel grateful and indebted to Aruna for sharing time with me. Her confidence in doing what is 'right' with India's women amazes me. Aware of the global nature of issues, she longs for all to recognize each

other and common pursuits. Aruna--involved on the national, Asian, and WCC scene--offers perspective on the interconnection between different organizations. Women, a real factor of hope for the world, together will discover and claim our strength.

"Herself comfortable with the term *feminist*, Aruna recognizes the need for Asians to develop distinct Asian meanings for it, or other terms.

"Aruna strongly opposes dowry. The church must denounce it, for either sons or daughters. Why the church does not confront such dehumanization of women (as property) pains Aruna. She advocates that women call leadership to refuse to perform marriages that include dowry. She told of a recent wedding in which the bride had joined her husband's family in requiring her family to give twenty-five thousand rupees, twenty-five pieces of gold, and extensive household furnishings. How some girls seem driven by materialism for definition deeply distresses Aruna...

"Aruna's really fine spirit pervades. She fully expects to bring about change within the church and among church leaders. I marvel at the approach of India's women leaders who proceed with confidence without arrogance--a real model for North American women."

[My later journal entry of May 30, 1990, reports again from Madras.]
"...We [Aruna, Lynda, and I] began our half-day together with a Chinese meal. Conversation topics varied--from differences between Orthodox (Syrian) and CSI (Church of South India); to the power of a single Orthodox bishop; to current writing and study efforts. Aruna recently addressed the all-Methodist women's [ten thousand] meeting in Kansas City, the only international speaker...She's editing a book about ecumenical issues and recently finished a chapter for another book.

"...Resistance comes in universal packages with men of any culture who wish not to credit women's strength...Aruna represents a good blend of keeping momentum moving while avoiding the overly-strident. Her strong sense of how to work with Roman Catholic, Orthodox, and Protestant women's groups reveals each group's strengths and limits. Further, she understands that, 'The common denominator of all religions is the spirit of non-acquisitiveness or the renunciation of Mammon [meaning total reliance on God]. Evangelical poverty is proclaimed in the Sermon on the Mount.'"

Aruna's compassionate theology appears also in her Christmas letters. With a footnote of explanation that followed, in 1995 she began:

We hold each other up in a circle of feminist power
And we stand here unflinching.
We stand here unafraid...
We look into each other's eyes with courage and energy,
A circle of life...of resilient power...and of love.

This is an extract from a poem I wrote a few months ago. It was inspired by the folk dance of many indigenous communities in India. In this dance, which is done to a simple rhythmic step and a simple melody usually sung by a group, what is significant is that the women hold each other around the waist and keep in a semi-circle, throughout the dance, never letting go of each other.

Aruna's rooted yet ever-branching theology dances on through her writing, more of which appears in Asian journals or publishers. Options for western readers include:

"A Spirituality that Sustains Us in Our Struggles," *International Review of Missions*, lxxx/317, Jan. 1991, 29-41.
"Born to her a son," in *New Eyes for Reading Biblical and theological reflections by women from the third world*, John S. Pobee and Barbel von Wartenberg-Potter, eds., Geneva:WCC 1986, 53-55.
"Feminist Theology: An Indian Perspective," *Asia Journal of Theology*, 2/1, Apr 1988, 109-118. (Also in *In God's Image*, Dec 1988, 44-51.)
Future of the Church in India, (editor), Nagpur:National Council of Churches in India, 1990.
"Sharing in the Signs of Hope," *International Review of Missions*, July 1984, 282-91.
"Women's Oppression: A Sinful Situation," in *With Passion and Compassion Third World Women Doing Theology*, Virginia Fabella and Mercy Amba Oduyoye, eds., New York:Orbis 1988, 69-76.

Part II. Inter-religious Dialogue: To Listen and Engage

For the main project of my recent Doctor of Ministry degree that focused on fostering inter-religious understanding, I created dialogues. One of them provides background for the daily encounter of women of varied living faiths in India. To be neighborly, one must know about and respect how others express the sacred. Imagined conversations are based on actual experience and informed writings; what follows is about one-third of one dialogue.

Two Indian women--Draupadi a Hindu and Darlene a Christian--have begun to co-chair a committee to implement more justice for women who live along the railroad tracks of their city. While their group endeavors will be oriented toward struggles of life, they realize that for them as leaders to invite each other to explain features of the religion they know best could assist their sense of working together. Listen in as their exchange begins.

Draupadi: Thanks for coming over. My twelve-year-old stayed home with a fever today, so I'm glad to meet here in case she calls.

Darlene: Our teenager mentioned yesterday that quite a few were missing from his classes, due to illness. In light of how close together people along the tracks live, and how soaked cloth and cardboard get during our monsoon showers, illness must spread in no time.

Draupadi: Such features of health will certainly be important for our women's group to process. I checked with my cousin who volunteers with an organization in her city. Preventive health measures are crucial to their program.

Darlene: I'm glad you have a resource like her to consult. The way women come together all over India to give each other support is really remarkable.

Draupadi: I also plan to send for materials from both SEWA and WWF.

Darlene: Good. Oh, that reminds me. My neighbor Kavi's father-in-law died yesterday in Chennai. She plans to leave on tonight's train; perhaps I could ask her to go directly to the Working Women's Forum office to request materials for us.

Draupadi: Would you do that at such a time, when people presume that extended family members are polluted by death? A key task for close relatives is to free the spirit of the dead. Further, they would be in a state of mourning for ten days.

Darlene: I hear your concern. But we Christians don't share all of your Hindu views about purity and pollution. So, Kavi could likely stop in at WWF a day or so after the burial.

Draupadi: Oh, yes. I guess we've already moved into our reason for meeting. Our religious practices will shape how we respond to or understand the "track" people.

As we acknowledge how religions devalue women or other oppressed people--whether through stereotypes, submission, or double standard--we'll be more alert to avoid self-denigrating comments if we hear them too.

Darlene: Also, I trust we'll be free to claim or reinforce liberating qualities of religion. To credit the spiritual dimension of courage and the will to survive as we see them demonstrated by friends along the tracks honors any faith.

Draupadi: By the way, are you comfortable with our calling those with whom we work "track" people, just because they live along the railroad tracks?

Darlene: I've wondered about that. Let's think seriously about other options.

Draupadi: I know the priest from the temple in that area. I'll ask him for counsel too.

Darlene: Back to your comment prior to my interruption about Kavi, thanks for writing to one of Ella Bhatt's workers with the Self-Employed Women's Association in Ahmedabad. Their community programs have been quite effective.

Draupadi: Adherents of most religions express faith through service to others. Motivation for service or how it is expressed might vary, but all faiths work to improve the quality of life.

Darlene: The struggle to cope with life is tougher for some than it is for others.

Draupadi: I marvel at the core qualities of those who meet obstacles. The struggle must seem endless, but their courage can shame mine.

Darlene: No doubt our new assignment will alert me to overlooked connections--how my actions affect another's options.

Draupadi: We'll need to avoid being patronizing as we build on the basic, human good that already rumbles alongside trains.

Darlene: You must hope also for a broad-based, humanitarian approach. I need to overcome the inclination to credit what is universal goodwill to a particular religion--mine. I fear that we Christians tend to claim service as our distinct quality, because of Jesus' example, but then fault Hindus for doing good simply to avoid negative consequences in the next life. I guess I'm apologizing to you.

Draupadi: Thanks for your honesty. Comparison of that sort could handicap our cooperative effort. I hear your wish to overcome an attitude that denies the best in others while claiming it for oneself.

Darlene: Thanks for understanding. Several Christian denominations practice a sacred rite, based on a teaching of Jesus', that symbolizes service by washing each other's feet.

Draupadi: Perhaps in certain climates to wash feet could be more symbolic. In rural India, especially prior to the rains, it can be ever so common.

Darlene: Might we develop a foot-washing ritual to greet each other? It could alternate with welcomes we already use in which we move our hands through the flame of fire held in a pan or have a *tilak* (dot) placed on our forehead, between the eyes.

Draupadi: Sounds creative and symbolic of inter-religious respect. I hope our group will design *kolams* (ground painting or writing) that transcend caste or a specific religion too.

Darlene: Do you know how the All India Women's Conference, founded in 1926, has promoted interfaith honor?

Draupadi: If you would check into that organization, I'll contact the Centre for Women's Development Studies (CWDS) in New Delhi with the same question.

Darlene: I knew a Christian woman who developed a severe back problem. Her Hindu landlady gave her a daily back rub--a sensitive act of service. Their friendship proved to be most genuine.

Draupadi: We seem to suggest that our volunteers could benefit from sharing about motives for program activities.

Darlene: We could prod each other always to foster self-worth in others, not dependency. To enhance each woman's sacred dream, whatever its Source.

Draupadi: I recall Mariasusai Dhavamony's definition of the deepest, most persistent aspiration of Hinduism: "a relentless quest for the inner experience and realization of the divine."

Darlene: We will value both inner experience and the empirical--rituals, social protest, or disciplined actions.

Draupadi: Reminders of the liberating strands and goals of all religions will be good to re-enforce too.

Darlene: As women, we know that religion has diminished us.

Draupadi: You Christians would admit that?

Darlene: Do I hear a slight tinge of critique? We aren't very honest about owning our faults to people of other faiths, I guess. Our illusion of "being better than Hindus" must be shed. For, yes, Christianity has both empowered and dis-empowered women.

Draupadi: Is that through laws, such as we inherited through Manu, the great Hindu lawgiver? Hindu thought instills a strong sense of duty; women or wives are always to be dependent on males--father, husband, or son. Our mythic example of the ideal woman is *Sita*, representative of the earth's prolific forces and consort of *Rama*.

Darlene: You mention myth. Each myth has multiple versions, doesn't it?

Draupadi: Of course. I value Shobita Punja's image: "Myths are an invitation to an inward journey...of self-discovery." Myths offer a way to communicate our community's sacred ideas.

Darlene: Do versions shift through time or because of you as an individual believer?
Draupadi: Both. They meet needs for adherents in different ways, simultaneously. Depending on a circumstance, we might tell our children features of a myth, to teach a concept. Storytelling is vital to Christian faith too, I'm sure.
Darlene: Yes, but we might presume less flexibility in re-telling an account. However, we likely don't realize how different our Indian version is from one in Zaire or New Zealand, or from liberation theology in Latin America.

You referred to *Rama*, the hero king of the *Ramayana* epic. I read recently, was it in *India Today*, about a Malaysia-based dance troupe that combines dances and concepts from all over to re-tell that epic. [Dec 31, 1996, 102]
Draupadi: Historian Romila Thapar explains how "floating" segments of the story change.

As the story traveled to a new area, the social structure of that area, the kin relations, ethnic relations, and belief structures of the people there influenced the way in which they reconstructed the story [to accord] with their own system of values and beliefs.

Darlene: Understandable. Nonetheless, despite injustices done, *Sita* remains loyal to her husband, as required by law.
Draupadi: Yes. Unfortunately, myth can be taken literally. I recommend that you read Punja's explanation about *Sita* as daughter of the earth. You evidently know of Sita's always putting *Rama's* welfare first. She worships him as metaphor for devotion to God.
Darlene: The *Ramayana* story, likely better known than any other among Hindus, includes banishment, abduction, and recapture, right?
Draupadi: Yes, but much more. The childless king Janaka finds an infant girl while plowing. He eventually sets up a contest to decide who will marry his beautiful princess. Only *Rama*, eldest son of King Dasaratha, succeeds in lifting and breaking the golden bow. But when Dasaratha pledges with a second wife that her son will inherit the throne, *Rama* is exiled to the forest.
Darlene: And utterly loyal *Sita* goes with him.
Draupadi: A demon woman, sister of ten-headed Ravana, king of Lanka, then tries to seduce *Rama*. She is avenged for his resistance when Ravana, sign of human greed and lust, forcefully kidnaps *Sita*. They fly in his chariot to Lanka.
Darlene: No wonder the story holds an audience captive.

Draupadi: Knowing the penalty for possessing a woman by force, Ravana offers to get rid of his other wives and give his wealth to *Sita*. Not impressed, she remains loyal to *Rama* despite Ravana's temptation, abuse, and threats.

Darlene: How often might some women along the tracks waver between enduring abuse from or remaining loyal to a husband. Features of this epic live ingrained through time.

Draupadi: More imagery surfaces as *Rama* and his brother secure a monkey army to form a bridge to Lanka to battle Ravana, whom *Rama* proceeds to kill. Having retrieved his *Sita*, *Rama* then doubts whether she remained faithful to him while in another's palace.

Darlene: And again, those who read or watch this story being depicted will choose. Choices include whether to feel empathy with *Sita's* agony for being rejected, to sense her obligation to preserve her husband's honor, or to endorse *Rama's* jealous renunciation of a woman.

Drampadi: *Sita* orders a fire to be lighted. She walks around it, calling on *Agni* the god of fire to intervene her plunge into the huge flame. Without hesitation, *Agni* verifies her purity.

Darlene: One would think the forces of good over evil had prevailed.

Draupadi: But on returning to Ayodhya, *Rama* yields to his imagination of the people's gossip. Moved by public censure, or placing the blame on others rather than assume personal responsibility, he banishes his pregnant *Sita* to a forest. She bears twin sons; when fifteen, the twins reunite with their father. *Sita* is invited to return also on condition that she once again proves her faithfulness through an ordeal by fire.

Darlene: How many, on hearing this epic recounted, wonder if *Rama* was faithful to *Sita* during their separations?

Draupadi: Have no fear! Conditioning prevails. But this time *Sita's* spirit will not comply. She draws the line, a line that some women along the parallel lines of steel track will comprehend. Endless injustice meets its consequence.

Interpreters vary. While Stella Faria believes that *Sita* shows *Rama* that he does not deserve her virtue, Sara Mitter suggests, "she sets her own terms for demonstrating her virtue." *Sita* states, "If I have never dwelt on any but *Rama*, may the Goddess [Earth] receive me!"

Darlene: Done with self-sacrifice and patience, she rebels. And the earth, in which she was found, receives her again as bold testimony. The tradition of long-suffering women devoted to their husbands continues to be glorified. Does the ideal of utter loyalty persist when the struggle to survive pervades?

Draupadi: Yes and no. We need to comprehend *Sita* also as *Shakti*, as that energy that motivates women because of what she represents. Our social action program might explore whether poverty increases or restricts a woman's religious being.

Darlene: You remind me of a study by Corinne Scott on "Poor Slum Women's Oppression and Sources of Strength..." I have several pages marked in my copy here, under "Religious Worldview."

Draupadi: I'd like to borrow that study.

Darlene: Sure. Scott says,

> ...a study of women's religious traditions and world views is important, in order to understand whether or not they provide validation of women, sources of energy or empowerment in women's lives, alternate cultural traditions, and sources of norms.

Draupadi: Validity, empowerment, traditions, and norms. Those are useful categories.

Darlene: She explains how goddesses are prominent in women's lives.

Draupadi: Of course. Five thousand years is a long time to provide influence. I suppose she discusses *Shakti* or female energy.

Darlene: From another resource about *Kali*, *Shakti* is described as "the energizing force of all divinity, of every being and every thing."

Draupadi: Yet, most living faiths ignore it, in part because of a patriarchal mentality.

Darlene: Religious principles often present a disjunction with social spheres. More popular or egalitarian religious options follow when a percentage of followers become dissatisfied with the long-established, elite, patriarchal base.

You likely know of the Brahma Kumari--Daughters of Brahma--sect founded fifty years ago. Disturbed by the Hindu ideal for a woman to consider her husband a deity, the Brahma Kumari founder stressed celibacy or that women should "transform their homes into 'temples.'"

Draupadi: What has been Christianity's more popular tradition for women?

Darlene: From what I know, our ancient Israelite heritage initially likely stemmed from a matriarchal epoch. Then, as a male God-concept endorsed by male priests gained strength, women's "place" within the cult diminished. For example, from not being <u>required</u> to attend special events, due in part to their sacred blood, women came to be <u>restricted</u> from being involved.

Exceptions always emerge. But dominant male authority figures have minimized those or posed women characters from an androcentric viewpoint. Fear of women and a need to justify social (patriarchal) patterns by reading back into the biblical text a male prerogative set the tone for centuries.

Draupadi: But change is taking place?

Darlene: Yes, too slowly or too rapidly, depending on one's stance.

Draupadi: That details of religions correspond is remarkable. Where protest begins, how tradition becomes further entrenched, or which outlasts the other are features to note.

Darlene: Back to *Sita's* example, have you read Savara and Thadani's *Reclaiming Female Energy*? I haven't, but Scott refers to this 1990 resource in stating: "in the many forms of *devi*, she is hardly ever seen as passive, obedient to father, husband or son." [67]

Draupadi: Fascinating. When women are conditioned to practice dependence, we neglect occasions to "reclaim female energy." However, nudged by vigorous efforts of survival, greater autonomy follows. I'm sure we'll return to this theme as we meet women along the tracks....

[After further dialogue, the two women agree on common concerns and the importance of mutual support. Rather than be isolated from each other because of faith, they choose to be open and honest about religious identity yet focus together in a primary way the task of overcoming oppression among the friends with whom they work for justice.]

11

From Coaldale to Jerusalem and Back

Kathy Bergen

* Jerusalem, the golden, city of my dreams, dreaming
how i waited all my life for you, to find you,
resplendent, in the sun, your white stones crying,
with joy, Jerusalem, beloved, lying in the
Mediterranean sun, filled with love, delirious
with love, lift up your heart and sing, my heart
dancing, how i longed for you, all my life, your
streets paved with gold, and children playing,
your diamond studded gates, your rooftops filled
with women, dancing, and flowers in their hair,
the tables laden, heavy, the air filled with music,
and feasting, my love, how i longed for you, dreaming,
my arms aching, from the day of my birth, my
birth-giving, filled with pangs of hunger and
remembering, how i longed for you, my love,
how long, oh how long i waited for you   * Poem by Di Brandt

During my first weeks in Jerusalem, in the fall of 1982, I remember
having an overwhelming feeling as I walked down Nablus Road towards
Damascus Gate--I have finally come home! I knew then that I would be
in Jerusalem for some time.

Places have become symbols of growth and landmarks on the
journey of life for me:

- Huenfeld--the place where I was born;
- Coaldale--the place where I grew up;
- Abbotsford--the first place I lived after leaving Coaldale;

- Calgary--university life and preparation for my career;
- Winnipeg--the place where I became aware of my Anabaptist heritage in a new way and my first grappling with social issues of justice and peace;
- Elkhart--the place of beginnings of the inner journey and where I recognized my gifts for ministry in the church;
- Jerusalem--the place where all the previous strands of my life met in the work I did and the people I knew;
- Geneva--continuation of commitment to justice and peace through the just cause of Palestinian people and my work in solidarity with them...
- Coaldale? Who knows?

Coaldale is what I call home. I have not lived there for many years, but it is the place where I have lived the longest. It is where I spent my most formative years. Coaldale--through family, church, schools, and community--has had a major influence on whom I have become. It is not my place of birth; that is Huenfeld. It is not the place of my family origins; that is Schoenhorst. It is not the place of origin of my church tradition; that is Zurich. It is not the place of origin of my faith tradition; that is Jerusalem. But it is the place to which I return--past, present, or future.

I see my life as a journey. Enroute, I have made many stops. In some places I have dwelt longer than others. Some stays have been short but significant; others served as a point of connection between two significant places.

The nine years I spent in Jerusalem symbolize for me integration--the coming together of many strands and finding a focus for moving beyond Jerusalem. The varied strands of life that came together there provided strength needed to give of myself. They convinced me of personal ability to learn. I want to speak of my years in Jerusalem from the perspective of being there as a woman, a Mennonite, and an international worker.

A. As a Woman in Jerusalem

As a woman, I lived in the shadow of many myths that have been perpetuated for generations. I tried to transcend these myths in my own ways. A North American man said to me soon after I began in Jerusalem: "Don't dump your North American ideas of women's liberation on the Palestinians."

Not until I attended the United Nations Decade for Women Conference in Nairobi in the summer of 1985--where I was part of a minority as a white and as a Canadian--was I able to see more clearly how similar women's issues are worldwide. The oppression of women takes distinct form in different countries, and ways of dealing with oppressions are culturally determined. But women's experience shares many features.

Within this spirit of commonality, I have learned about the specific issues that Palestinian women face. I have become supportive of the women of Palestine in whatever way possible.

Palestinian women are part of a traditional and male-oriented society that is struggling for national liberation. These three factors, plus others, make the struggle for Palestinian women difficult and complex. Each is constantly at play, vying for the forefront of women's attention. Only within the last ten or so years have women named the social and gender struggle to be of equal importance with the national agenda.

Palestinian women are struggling on three fronts.

1. On the gender front, Palestinian women face a traditional, male-oriented society with overwhelming expectations. A woman is expected to fulfill all the traditional roles of wife, mother, and homemaker. In this context women try to find their place as productive, equal members of society. One concern of Palestinian women is the absence of choice--whether to follow a traditional or non-traditional role. If a woman chooses a role in the workplace, she is often expected to fulfill all the traditional roles of women in addition to employment. In order to be credible and equal to her male counterparts in the professional world, she must be a "superwoman."

2. On the social front, Palestinian women face a traditional class-oriented society. Status is not only determined by education acquired and the amount of money that education provides. Family of origin and the amount of land and money a family has traditionally held also shape this.

3. On the national front, Palestinian women struggle alongside their men for national and political rights, for self-determination of their people. Men have validated women's efforts alongside men in the struggle to liberate Palestine. The Palestinian women's multi-faceted struggle continues to challenge women's movements around the world, including the Israeli women's movement. Women from the two movements have interacted. Palestinian women say to Israeli women, How can you struggle for your own liberation as women and not see the equally valid Palestinian struggle? Such honesty and interaction has caused many Israeli women to respond to their Palestinian sisters in their own way.

To know Palestinian women and some of their struggles has challenged some of my perceptions as a white, middle class western woman. Knowing of women's struggles within other cultures forces me to re-evaluate who I am and my struggles. The interplay of learning from and giving to those around me gives me energy to continue my work and commitments.

B. As a Mennonite in Jerusalem

I came to Jerusalem with the identity of a Mennonite working in a Mennonite institution. "Mennonite" meant different things to the people whom I encountered every day. But for me it was a way of being there that felt secure, familiar and right. I knew who I was and why I was there. I could have been anywhere in the world involved in justice and peace ministry. But I had chosen to live in Jerusalem and to work with Palestinians in the West Bank and Gaza Strip (Occupied Palestine).

I was motivated by a biblical, Anabaptist perception of justice and peace. My strength came from knowing that I was in the right place, at the right time, doing the right thing. I knew this through the feedback I had from people around me and from the inner peace I felt through prayer, meditation and reflection.

My growth--definite stretching and learning--came when I was forced to continue my life and work in this place where I felt drawn, but outside the framework of an institution of my faith commitment. After deep soul-searching, I realized that I could continue to do the same work, with the same sense of profound commitment, but within the context of an institution that did not articulate its framework in the same terms as a church institution. I had worked in "secular" institutions earlier and had not experienced inner conflict. This time, I further intuitively knew that I had integrated my Anabaptist Mennonite identity in a new way--Jerusalem, Zurich, Winnipeg and Elkhart had come together.

C. As an International Worker

I began my work in Jerusalem knowing that I had something to give and much to learn. Both of these facts became increasingly true as my time in Jerusalem progressed.

I learned a lot about oppression. Increasingly aware of the oppression of the Palestinians made me more keenly aware of my own oppression. Further, I learned how I as a North American was part of a society and a network of systems that oppress peoples around the world. This interplay of greater awareness of being oppressed plus a keener ownership of personal involvement in oppressing others became very delicate to sort through at times.

Oppression is ugly--it dehumanizes the oppressed and the oppressor. Oppression solicits violent responses from the oppressed. Feelings of powerlessness give way to anger, which in turn can lead to empowerment or to a sense of helplessness. Hopelessness can give way to hatred and bitterness. I discovered that oppression takes many forms. But it differs little whether perpetrated by a government, an institution, or an individual.

On the one hand, as an international, I received direct and indirect messages from the Palestinians. "Get out and leave us alone," for example. On the other hand: "We need you; you have something to offer to us." I believe that both messages are sincere. Palestinians had to articulate them and I had to hear both. They helped me to continually evaluate why I was there, and what I was doing there.

Not until my sixth year of living and working in Jerusalem, did I experience a new and revolutionary change in my relationship to the Palestinians. I had come to Jerusalem to work with the Palestinians. Suddenly I needed them more than they needed me. During this time of need, they expressed solidarity with me--at the same time when very involved in their own struggle. Despite the latter, they gave me unsolicited support when I most needed it. We had become partners!

I next lived and worked in Geneva, another stop on the journey. Again, I learned a lot. Again I drew on my past in order to do the work required. It stretched me in areas and in directions I could not have imagined years prior.

The ICCP (International Coordinating Committee for Non-governmental Organizations on the question of Palestine) is a coordinating body for approximately one thousand NGOs and four hundred individuals. From around the world, these are involved, in some way, in the question of Palestine or in solidarity with the Palestinian people.

As the Executive Secretary of the ICCP, I tried to implement important principles of leadership germane to such an office:

1. I shared as much information with the persons working in the office, and with the ICCP Board, as I could.

2. I shared as much of the decision-making process as possible with everyone in the office.

3. I tried to create an open atmosphere where everyone could contribute and in which everyone's gifts were valued and used.

4. I tried to create an atmosphere where the NGOs and individuals who are part of the ICCP network could be enabled, through this office, to

better do their own work related to Palestine and solidarity with the Palestinian people.

5. I initiated ideas, projects, and decisions where I feel they were useful.

In conclusion, I am asked: "With all the moving you have done, don't you feel like you need to put down roots somewhere? Where is your home?"

Yes, perhaps I will become more rooted. But I choose to look at my life experiences as having provided a home and a family for me in the many places where I have lived.

----

* Di Brandt is a Canadian poet of Mennonite origin who has lived in Winnipeg, Manitoba, Canada. A long-time friend, she and her two daughters, Lisa and Alison, visited me in Jerusalem as I was about to leave there. They provided a significant link for me from the past to the future by being present during an important time of transition.

12

A Poetic Turn

Jean Gerber

Appetizers   (Excerpts from a larger collection)   (In respect to Norge)

mothers
Have a hard time biting a piece of day to themselves. Jackknives, shoestrings, knots in feelings to untie, scribbled rays of suns, a tower block glory, dishes and muddy boots, splinters and odorous cries. After a number of years get downright hungry.

portrait
Take a goldfish from the side and it speaks of eloquence, frothing grace, a caressing pace. But head-on what a pursed-up glare. Like a nail lined up to hammer or a look through the keyhole where one's view stops up short. If I ever chance to pose for you, please draw me from my best side.

mango
A mess of juice runs down the chin. Choose the small round orange ones rather than the elite ovals in their green and red casing that with knife and fork linger sculpted on the plate. The bulge at the southern hemisphere hangs hot. A black hand cups an orange egg. The noonday sun aha! caught in sweet strings between the teeth.

racing
We race cars, bikes, skis, horses, patents and getting to the moon. We pay money to watch it all happen. But the race I remember best I saw for free, on a green-dotted hillside in the Caribbean Sea. At the signal the women jumped into action, skirts flapping red, orange and blue in the rush. They sliced knives deftly left and right, hitting the heads with one sure deadening thud, piling their own in an odd-shaped stack. Shouts of glee glinted off the knives like sunrays until the whistle

shrilled, marking the end of the cabbage field harvest.   A crouched
leisurely wait for the count.   Paid per whacked head.

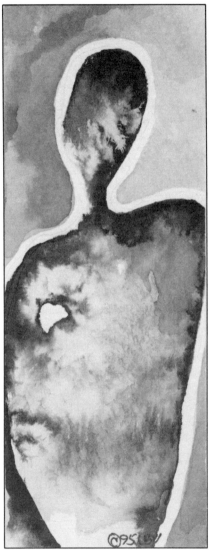

women
Sit   well.
They   make
room   for
arms.   Their
eyes   listen
while   their
ears see. You
can enter their
downtown
from   many
directions.
Don't   hurry
so.   They are
not afraid of
winter and are
familiar   with
odors   of   all
kinds. Do not
be surprised if
there   is   a
glove of anger
under   their
skin.

men
Do not know
what they are
missing.   In
their
excitement to
open the door
they see only
their own entrance.   Their lying is usually harmless except when
it is to themselves.   If they took the back seat more often
perhaps the car would run on less gas.   But they do make a
fascinating   stampede.   Tick tock, the sturdy chair of a
grandfather. A rough hand laid soft.

recipes
Are waiting to be invented. We're talking of basic ingredients. Instead of flour, try air; instead of sugar, whistling; instead of egg, fire. Let the tears flow. Let the angel turn the spoon.

N-S-E-W
It must be hard to be a tram. Doesn't choose much. Has to constantly stay connected (above), follow repeated advice (below). May be able to stop and start at will, ring a bell, let off a spark or two. But it sure can't choose much.

Benedictine sisters
Don't let their tan dress fool you. Underneath they come in oh such colors. This one walks towards me with bright red wings and shoes that bounce like new growth in spring. Her old hands are solidly rooted in the earth. Holding Christ's feet caked in mud. Oh the questions she dares to give wing to. Nothing is off her map, and when I walk out the monastery door the world has gone wide. An unidentifiable new taste on the tongue.

manna
Is enough if its sustenance you're searching for and if you pick up the appropriate amount daily. Some need more, some less. Sift it slowly through the fingers; admire its airy way of filling in. Those who tire of its' linger on the tongue, who turn up their noses saying "what is it?" as on the first day it came down to them, need their memory jarred. They've forgotten the lashes down the backs, the thunder of the chariot's wheels and the beasties that troubled the airs all round--the price Egypt had to pay. This is a time of daily exercises, of little gestures: pulling up the tent pegs, folding the cloth, filling the jar and setting the eyes on the cloud that moves ahead, the fire in the dark.

Disciple

She wants to follow
with the patient migratory memory of the elephant.
At the familiar tug
she winds her trunk around the tail in front

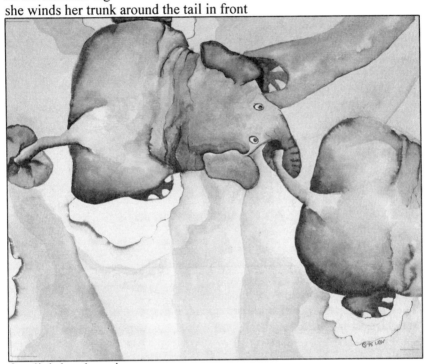

feet lightly advancing
without raising much dust.

Water wells, cool sulky forests pocket her head
like flowers opening in slow motion.
The heart beats, a steady pulse as sure as roots
traveling in tendrils through readied ground.
As the sun rises the day leads the meandering line to an
abundance of swaying grasses and hardy leaves.
The line gives way like a
kaleidoscope forming a new pattern
on the savanna floor.

Ears talk as well as hear--yes,

she flaps them to call her young
who nuzzles at her nipples, at rest in the
yawn of her enormous bulk.
She sways, ah...the soft heavy slowness of her as an
egret alights on her back.

The nose feels as well as smells—yes
exploring, snuffling along the wrinkled gray skins
taking in familiar, reassuring news.
She caresses the head of an old friend,
taps her young one on its shoulder,
reaches up to haul on a tree branch with a rough power
like the lick of a cat's tongue.
Forty-thousand muscles in that swirl of a nose
(not that she's ever bothered to take count).

The tightness of her own skin,
the glint of the water yet untouched
calls to the midday festivity: a guzzling of drinks,
straws bubbling ridiculously,
a gush of spouts on heads and backs.
Lumbering crackled skins begin to glisten black
like oiled machines eager to work
like testimonies to muddy baptisms.
They let themselves fall--unrestrained side-claps of
satisfaction.

Lying on her side among them, trunk lightly lifted to
catch the slightest breeze
she knows that there is no other moment
other than this one.
Her flank mounts: up, down.

Her little one clambers out, lies down,
sucking his trunk like a thumb.
The sky indicates no danger.
Ten kilometers away a kindred group signals that they too
are at rest.

Here, in this water hole, she only faintly recalls the dry years,
the moments of terror as the flames licked her back—
the ambling head low when hole after hole is found dry

and the trunk reaches down into one's own stomach
to pull out a precious liquid for life—oh
the parched eye, the skin that has nowhere to go—
She ate dirt then as now, minerals dusted into her
empty stomach but it
was not enough.

She does not recall,
or if she does, she spreads the memory far out
into her network of weight.
She stands,
water wealthy, shining steep,
    --because her memory leads her forward—

The matriarch calls them once more into line.
Tails lead as well as follow.

Walk among bones or A tribute to Ezekiel who was not afraid of charades

The bones come together with a great clattering.
A whacking clamor for attention.
In the midst of it I am a living anomaly.
A confused warmth of blood
        dropped into a skipping gale of white and tan.
It is a prolonged mad scramble, with fainter clicks and
        snaps as the final smaller bones slip into place.

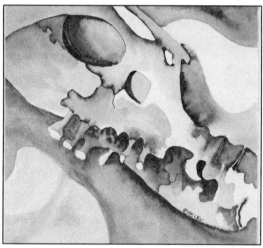

A great stillness descends.

I lift a goblet to my lips.
The sinews begin to grow. A faint but eager sound like thirsty
        ground soaking up water.
A dizzy humming sets in and the vigor of life in growth thrumbs me
        with a grotesque bewildering
Is this what we are made of?

                One would almost rather not know.
                Leave it to the surgeons.
                There, in antiseptic chambers, others view the
                Altars of our insides.

Is this what we are made of?
We have been carried to the valley.
Flesh takes many turns.
I cannot tear my eyes away.
It is an army.
A battle of returning life.
I stand as a statue among
the groaning of things long past rearranging themselves
Standing up in a glory
that is yet to be theirs.

The valley expanse has turned red and brown, black and white
with the writhing of sinews and flesh.
The sun, rising, brings out unknown tints in the countless skins
At an invisible signal they come to shining attention
Rooted in their newly found position.
Waiting for the breath.
For the prophet and the four winds.

From where will come the breath?
Who will call it to the fore?
And if, as I presume, you too have been carried here
In what part of this valley do you set your feet?

(Untitled)

The water jug will be lifted to her shoulder
and step after step the narrow path
will carry her up.
Switching weight around boulders and crags
she scans the air a great effort all around
until a level stretch
sets her hips to a rhythmic rest
such as the cradle rock
of huge arms from above.

She will not stop.

Greening keening birds beckon and will fill
the sky with great sunset longing
with a fullness too large for her
skirt and apron eyes
but the feet and the ankles furrow their way
praying out their path
echoing a plusty drumbeat
in the fountain of her heart.

For the water jug has been to the fountain.
She has hiked it onto her shoulder
and she does not know
where
to set
it down.

[Batik created by
Gretchen Nyce, 1986]

Medley

do)
Where to perch my pride?
I have tried hanging its hollowed triangular shape
on the tip of my nose
where it glows
        but mostly I stick it in pockets.

I have balanced it haphazardly
on the edge of the hip
a precarious fit
        but mostly I stick it in pockets.

I have hidden it like a gem in the corner of my eye
and tucked it deftly at the edge of my hat.
I have soothed it, combed its snarls out of my hair,
Lain it flat in the palm of my hand--
        but often it lies, oddly misplaced
        in the bottoms of pockets.

re)
    P-R-I-D-E. I count mine up carefully, stacking the coins in neat little
piles. Rather meager, but it will have to do. I set 10% aside as a tithe,
another 20% for taxes and count out 10% as a loan for my friend Juanna.
I hand over 10% to my husband for safe keeping, put 20% down for a
land purchase for sowing poems, spend 10% battling pubic opinion, give
4% to each of the children for their allowance, 1% for postage stamps
for writing old acquaintances and drop the final few coins into the
bottom of my pocket.

mi)
When I move
to the tam-tam
coins start appearing
out of my ears
and between my toes
dropping from my belly button

When I swim
they slowly start to shine like
scattered mermaid scales

on my legs
collect in my bathing cap and
fall out of the folds of my towel

Sometimes I discover extra coins
jingling in my pocket
simply by rounding a corner
shaking a hand or
smiling unexpectedly
into the jaws of the crocodile.

la)
It is not necessary to be a flower.
A little moss growing slowly in the crux of the wall
will do.
A puddle rippling slightly in the wind,
evaporating in the patient stare of the sun
only to disappear
is enough.

The whiff of your name
has been spoken out loud
already
and is traveling outwards
at incredible speed
expanding the universe.
The beat of your heart
that has seethed like red-hot lava
is slowly cooling into tender graffiti
inside a mountain
near your home.

Your sliver of glory
does not need to be daily shined like silver
or polished like shoes.
If you turn those pockets inside out
a dust of gold will sift off
buzzing softly
like homing bees.

(Untitled)

Moving on towards the end of the century
she chooses to take large slow strides
though any pace could suit for
there is always just the right amount of time.
The year has taught her that we fit easily
into eternity.
Every name is knotted to the alpha and the omega.
The sounds we make when night comes
fall into a willing bed.

Our bodies wash up on the shore
of the percussive currents of time
bearing marks: tender wrinkles, dimples, scratches, scars, stigmata.
She, for instance, runs her hand over stomach stretch marks,
a be-riddled fingerprint of her works of birth.
The evasive lines fill her with
neither pride nor shame
but rather with an odd wonder
for they speak less of her
than of the growth of the one who came forth,
the unrelenting drive towards the first breath,
the gift
that never
depended
on her
own
effort.

13

Ye forest leaves, so green and tender,
That dance for joy in summer air."
Johann Mentzer

Hope and Liberation

Manini Nayar Samarth

Although the inward turn of fiction, the genre of the psychological novel, has been studied extensively in western literature, this mode of fiction has been only marginally discussed in the context of the Indian novel in English. The turn inward in Indian fiction in English has arisen primarily since Independence [1947] with the works of Anita Desai, Arun Joshi, and Kamala Markandaya, among others. For the description of the motivations that led to the formation of the internalized narrative in English, an inquiry into the historical framework from which it developed proves relevant.

The novel in the western world is primarily concerned with time and space and their effects on humanity. The novelist is less concerned with eternal absolutes and their presentation in a timeless setting. The concern is more with the description of historical humanity within the flux of society and politics. Unlike poetry, which explores "eternal truths" and can be suspended in space and time, the modern novel is an organic product of a particular society at a given time.

Since the novelist's subject is a person-in-society, the Indian writer in *Indian languages* has better access to the manners, customs and traditions by which a social person's identity is defined. That the earliest novels in India were written in the vernacular is hardly surprising. Indo-Anglian novelists, on the other hand, exist simultaneously in two worlds: they speak an acquired and alien language to interpret the values and experiences of a lived context. Meenakshi Mukherjee argues in *The Twice Born Fiction* that for the Indian novel in English to develop in the wake of the Indian novel in the vernacular is a logical progression. Both kinds of fiction may be categorized in three successive stages: 1) the historical romance, 2) novels of social and political realism, 3) the introspective novel. (19)

The historical romances and novels of realism belong to Frantz Fanon's second phase of de-colonization described in *The Wretched of the Earth.* In this period the subject colony rises in revolt against the colonizer's oppression (222). R. Taranath and S. Tharu argue that the earliest examples of Indo-Anglian poetry (Toru Dutt, Henry Derozio) were imitative of western romantic models. However, the Indo-Anglian novels of the early 1900's are associated with the awakening of Indian nationalism.

The turn of the century romances, like S.K. Shosh's *The Prince of Destiny* or a later work like A.S. Aiyyar's *Baraditya* [1930], imply a safe form of patriotism through the celebration of past glory. Taranath points out that with the moral fervour generated by the Indian National Congress and Mahatma Gandhi, expressions of nationalism grew bolder. Mulk Raj Anand's progressivism and Raja Rao's Gandhian zeal established social realism as the prevalent mode of Indo-Anglian fiction in the 1940's.

While the historical and realistic novels are variants of patriotic rebellion coinciding with Fanon's second phase, his prophesied third phase of a literature that incites the masses into awareness of "a new reality in action" (223) has been slow to develop. Instead, as Mukherjee argues, the trend after Independence is toward introspection. This moves toward shaping a private reality in the attempt to assume a coherent sense of self.

After Independence, as Taranath points out, an important stimulus for heroic action disappeared. No longer a patriot spokesman for a community, the Indo-Anglian writer had to redefine the terms of personal existence without an external focus to give it meaning. Hence, the turn inward, or the need to reconstruct the self through the imagination rather than from a basis in patriotism and moral fervour.

Anita Desai, [1937--], among the best known "inward turning" novelists today, has at least ten novels and a collection of short stories to her credit. She was nominated for Britain's coveted Booker prize in 1978 and 1984, and has been awarded India's Sahitya Academy Award for literature. A Fellow of the Royal Society of Literature, Desai won the Winifred Holtby prize for her fifth novel, *Fire on the Mountain.*

Desai resolves her almost mystical quest for synthesis between the self and the world through her fiction. Her protagonist is usually an alter self, a persona, whose inner life serves as the subject of the novel. Into this the external world is absorbed and redefined. Action is internalized. What *happens* is of less significance than how the person's consciousness develops through understanding her experiences. The point of aesthetic closure in Desai's novels usually coincides with the resolution of the flow of consciousness in a moment of epiphany. Her novels thus attempt to bridge the self and the world, as the persona recognizes her oneness with all things through heightened revelation.

Bim, in *Clear Light of Day*, is among Desai's most independent and effective protagonists. She even serves as a blueprint of sorts--with a few exceptions--for the central character in each of Desai's novels. *Clear Light of Day* opens by establishing various contrasts of character within the structure of a decaying family house in Old Delhi. The place is now "dead and stale," with memories of illness and death. Here Bim, an unmarried, middle-aged professor lives with her retarded younger brother Baba. She shares with him a life of comfortable tedium.

Into this placid existence comes the sensitive and highly-strung younger sister, Tara. She had escaped the stifling hold of the house through marriage to Bakul, a pompous bureaucrat. Tara's return opens old wounds, forcing Bim to review the past as a living force that influences the present and shapes the future. Tara's return, in this way, articulates the thematic concern of the novel: the continuity of time which neutralizes and absorbs conflicts into a single, fluid harmony.

The past surfaces first as a threat to Bim's quiet existence. It attempts to undermine her courage and practical wisdom in emotional re-plays of hurtful memories. But, unlike Tara, Bim is too strong to succomb. Tara is plagued with guilt for abandoning her sister to the living grave of a decrepit, sorrow-laden house. Her guilt is symbolically compressed onto a childhood incident when Tara abandoned Bim to swarms of attacking bees at a picnic.

Bim's initial response to Tara's need to expiate her guilt combines irritation with anger. Aware that she was always the less attractive and more aggressive sister, Bim remembers having vied with Tara for their brother Raja's attention. Yet, Raja, the Byronic Urdu poet of the family, betrayed the sisters' faith in him by eloping after Independence with Benazir, their Muslim landlord's daughter. Worse, he had humiliated Bim with a patronizing letter, one from a new landlord to his favoured tenant. Feeling abandoned by her sister and brother, orphaned early and scornful of men, Bim develops a protective, iron independence.

Since much of the present is filtered through Bim's perceptions, she is clearly the novelist's persona. Yet she remains a much stronger and determined central character than any of Desai's preceding protagonists. The nature of the change in character and consciousness indicates a progressive movement from despairing inaction (Maya in *Cry, the Peacock*; Sita in *Where Shall We Go This Summer?*) to the ability to act in loss and suffering.

Yet the progress is partial. Bim is still a fragmented character, unable to justify her bitterness toward family betrayals and their parasitical dependence on her. All these years, Bim "had felt herself the centre" and Tara, Bakul, Raja and Benazir had "come like mosquitoes" only "to torment her...to sip her blood." (153) In a flash of anger, she lashes out at the quiet, retarded Baba haplessly playing his old records. She suggests that he live with Raja, so that at last Bim might live in peace, without responsibility.

But Bim realizes at once the cruelty of her threat. For, Baba's "silence and reserve and unworldliness she wanted to break open and ransack and rob...." (164) In this sudden recognition of her deepest need for spiritual silence, Bim sees that she is very like Tara. "...they were, more alike than any two people could be." (180) Despite herself, Bim begins to realize her connectedness with people she had wanted to dispense with.

She sees now that Tara's return bridges the past, present and future. It is the catalyst that stirs her consciousness into an active, spiritual involvement with the world. No longer can she exist in isolation, protecting her frayed spirit with solitude. Her consciousness is impelled toward vision. Bim sees that her family and friends "were all part of her, inseparable, so many aspects of her as she was of them, so that the anger and disappointments she felt in them" were nothing more than "the anger and disappointments she felt at herself." (165)

At this point, Bim's rationally-derived sense of oneness is still "shadowy and dark," distanced from actual experience. She tells herself she must forgive Raja his betrayal, give Tara the forgiveness she seeks, and ask forgiveness from Baba for her gratuitous cruelty to him. She must dissolve all conflicts in love, just as temporal boundaries dissolve in a single Bergsonian continuum. But her awareness is rational, not instinctual, and the means of such perfect love seem beyond her grasp.

Yet knowledge descends on Bim, almost in an act of grace, at the novel's closure when Bim attends a musical soiree. The image of the two contrasting musicians offers Bim a moment of epiphany that unifies her life into a "wholeness" that is "perfect." (166) She sees in the difference between the old musician and the younger singer a formal representation of her own contradictory experience:

> The contrast between Mulk's voice and his was great: whereas Mulk's voice had been almost like a child's, so sweet and clear, or a young man's, full and ripe with a touch of sweetness to it, the old man's was sharp, even a little cracked, inclined to break, although not merely with age but with the bitterness of his experiences, the sadness and passion and frustration....He sang like a man who had come to the end of his journey, within sighting distance of death so that he stood already in its looming presence and measured the earth and his life by the great shadow. (182)

Like Bim and her siblings, the musicians are diametrically opposed in their music. Yet they remain indivisibly connected at the source, rooted in the same history and traditions: "there was this similarity despite the great gulf between them." (182) The contradictory images of Mulk and his guru--each singer representing the dual aspects of time, and of character and perceptions--is synthesized in one ancient school of music.

Bim realizes that her brothers and sister view life like children. Their perceptions are "sweet and clear" and "full and ripe," with the innocence of those who focus only on their immediate concerns. Baba will continue to play his old records, Tara to quest for affection, Raja to indulge in poetry. But she, Bim, taking her cue from the tenor of the old man's voice, remains "sharp" and "inclined to break" with the "bitterness" of past losses. The "sadness and passion and frustration" of unrealized hopes and forgotten dreams continue to haunt Bim in a way that Baba, Raja and Tara will never know.

Bim, like the old singer, stands apart from the family. So much spiritually older than they, she stands "within sighting distance of death." Mystically transported to this point of awareness through song, Bim's epiphanic knowledge is foreshadowed in her description of the old man "at the end of his journey." She too nears her spiritual journey's end. The moment when she will redefine her past existence. The point by which she can "measure her life on earth." Bim knows now that

> her own house and its particular history linked and contained her as well as her own family with all their

separate histories and experiences--not binding them within some...airless cell, but giving them the soil in which to send down their roots, and food to make them grow and spread, reach out to new experiences and new lives, but always drawing from the same soil, the same secret darkness. The soil contained all time, past and future, in it. It was where her deepest self lived, and the deepest selves of her sister and brothers, and all those who shared that time with her. (182)

The image of the singers as balanced contradictions, dual halves of a whole, is Bim's own history and that of her family as harmonized oppositions. The house becomes for Bim an organic, living metaphor nourishing their lives. The house is the nurturing base from where the family "grows and spreads," a shared referent for emotional sustenance.
The added implications of "secret darkness" connect the metaphor with the subconscious and the primeval. The family's emotional bond, the image suggests, goes beyond conscious awareness, and is rooted deeply in the blood. Also, an image of primeval slush from which all life arose, the "secret darkness" implies that their love both "contains all time" and is beyond time. A bond of the soul that both contains and precedes all existence. The connotative range of the house-imagery is reinforced by the implications of the contrasted darkness/light images. From darkness the family grows into the light of "new experiences, new lives," just as the primal organism, created in darkness, evolves in light.
With her deepest self now brought into focus, Bim experiences the joy and peace she had earlier only intuited in her responses to Baba. Aware at last, first rationally, and now wholly, through visionary experience, of the continuity of life and the unity of all things, Bim is freed at last of anxiety and anger. At the closure, the sacramental image of the old man's uplifted hand is Desai's benediction to Bim, her persona, to go in peace. Having involved herself in life, however transient, having kept courage and hope, Bim, though still alone in the "ocean of life," progresses toward a happy and fulfilled death. Her mystical vision finds expression in the words of the 17th Mughal emperor, Aurangazeb, that come to her as a prayer:

Many were around me when I was born, but now I am going alone. I know not why I am nor wherefore I came into the world....Life is transient and the lost moment never omes back....When I have lost hope in myself, how can I have hope in others? Come what will, I have launched my frail bark upon the waters." (168)

Aurangazeb's farewell has become Bim's truth, uniting time past and present into an indivisible flow. The "net" made whole, the bark launched in peace, now Bim is perfected, her spirit "stilled at last." Mystic love, the synthesis of the self and world, the unity of being--these are the themes that set Desai apart from more mainstream contemporary Indo-Anglian novelists. Though not overtly religious, her works seem almost a metafictional representation of her own quest for secular harmony. Like Bim, Desai invests her spirit in the here and now, seeing how each moment is inherently sacred, potentially liberating and fulfilling, if only we cared to pause and question the small and bitter conflicts of our lives.

Works Cited

Desai, Anita. *Clear Light of Day*. New Delhi:Allied Publishers, 1980.

Fanon, Frantz. *The Wretched of the Earth*. New York:Grove Press, 1956.

Mukherjee, Meenakshi. *The Twice Born Fiction: Themes and Techniques of the Indian Novel in English*, New Delhi:Arnold Heineman, 1971.

Taranath, R. and S. Tharu. Seminars at CIEFL, Hyderabad, India. 1980.

[The author wishes to thank S. Tharu and R. Taranath for information on the historical motivations for Indian writing in English.]

14

"Canst thou prophesy, thou little tree,
What the glory of thy boughs shall be?" Lucy Larcom

Grief and Healing: Abortion and *Mizuko Kuyô* in Japan

Mary Beyler

Bibbed and capped Jizo statues with their colorful charm and cuteness have caught my attention and aroused my curiosity from my first travels around Japan. However, I was puzzled by the embarrassed reactions and vague answers received whenever I asked Japanese friends about their purpose. Nor was I satisfied with the simple answer from guidebooks, dictionaries, or friends: that Jizo is the guardian deity of children and travelers. Only after I could read and speak Japanese for myself did I find out that a vast majority of the Jizo statues were actually connected with *mizuko kuyô*, memorial services for abortions, miscarriages, stillbirths, and babies who died shortly after birth.

The *mizuko kuyô* phenomenon

> Represents emotional problems encountered by large numbers of Japanese women following an abortion experience, and efforts by Buddhism and other religious groups in Japan to respond to these problems.[1]

Because of the breakdown of the traditional family and community support system in contemporary Japan, responsibility for abortion "must be borne in secret completely by the individual."[2]

> It is precisely this "broken connection"...that needs examining, not only with respect to earlier family systems and communal forms of support but also compared with former ways of relating death to life.[3]

Recent research confirms that

> the problems experienced through abortion in Japan are not only more serious than is often acknowledged, but that complex factors related to abortion exist within Japanese society which are rarely discussed.[4]

This paper will look at the emotional response of contemporary Japanese women to abortion, as shown in the growing popularity of *mizuko kuyô*. It explores whether *mizuko kuyô* helps to heal negative reactions attributed to abortion.

Abortion

Abortion has been legal in Japan since the Eugenic Protection Law was introduced in 1948, with subsequent liberalization steps in 1949 and 1952. Japan's abortion rate is high, worldwide, but abortion is practiced "in a social context of reproach"[5] Although easily available and legally permitted, abortion is less acceptable religiously, socially and emotionally.

Affecting how acceptable abortion is in Japan is the generally known Buddhist belief that life begins at conception.

> The pervasiveness of this teaching may perhaps be seen in the negligible influence on Japan of the modern western tendency to rationalize when the fetus becomes a 'person' on physiological grounds.[6]

As Buddhist priest Miura says, "Once a child has received life it surely begs to be allowed to be born."[7]

Is there a contradiction between this widespread regard for the value of life and prevalent abortion? Buddhist literature clearly opposes abortion. However, established Buddhism has been slow to voice opposition.[8] This contradiction can be explained by considering bi-level Japanese thought: *tatemae* (theoretical) and *honne* (practical).

> On a theoretical level, Japanese oppose abortion, but on a practical level they realize they must face the realities of life: an unexpected pregnancy, limited living space, or financial problems, for example.[9]

Thus, abortion is perceived as a necessary evil, not ideal. It is one of the unavoidable dilemmas of life.

Unlike in the U.S., where women around age twenty have the greatest number of abortions, Japanese women around thirty form the major group. The 25-29 and 30-34 age groups accounted for 51.8 percent of the total number of abortions in 1981.[10] Statistics reveal that the average Japanese married woman experiences two abortions.[11]

This high rate of abortion among married women cannot be explained only by the fact that abortion is accessible and legal. Other available methods of birth control are inadequate. Modern contraceptive methods are not encouraged or easy to obtain. Birth control information and counseling are insufficient. Physicians appear to be "less committed to pregnancy prevention than to pregnancy termination."[12] A marketing system "has developed the largest and most innovative condom distribution program in the world."[13] To discuss sexual relations remains a taboo in most circles, sometimes between husband and wife. Japanese women lack sufficient choice in birth control and suffer "an alarming rate of unwanted pregnancies within marriage."[14]

As long as present patterns of birth control continue and abortion remains an option for unwanted pregnancy, women will reluctantly choose abortion as one of the few options open to them. "The decision to abort is not often made, however, without regret, guilt, trauma and--increasingly--fear of mizuko curse."[15]

Besides the universal emotions of grief and guilt experienced with abortion, the Japanese worldview adds a particular emotion--anxiety or fear about *mizuko* curse. "Regardless of the motivations underlying the practice of abortion in contemporary Japan, Japanese in general cannot escape having some bad feelings about aborting a child."[16] For, abortion violates the Buddhist principle of respect for life accepted by most Japanese. Also,

> the tendency even today among many Japanese to non-rational or non-scientific habits of investigating cause and effect may produce in some Japanese anxiety about the potential danger of the unmemorialized souls of aborted babies. [17]

Hoshino and Takeda also mention cause-effect thinking:

> Abortion in contemporary Japan is not unavoidable or necessitated by natural calamity, but is carried out by individual will in the midst of material prosperity, against a child whose probability of dying before reaching maturity is otherwise extremely low, and who

has become "humanized" in contemporary society. This results in a feeling of indebtedness and self-recrimination and a search for a cause and effect relationship which finds the reason for one's happiness or unhappiness in the fact of an abortion. In addition, anxiety of a possible curse from an aborted baby, based on this feeling of indebtedness, comes from the...development that children are now considered as being in the same category as adults...and thus have the potential for casting a curse.[18]

Hoshino and Takeda distinguish between abortion and infanticide as practiced in traditional Tokugawa (1600-1868) society and abortion as practiced today.[19] They suggest reasons for the fear of *mizuko* curse. First, pregnancy was common, public knowledge in the communal Tokugawa period. Today it is a private affair. Second, abortion was earlier dangerous, often life-threatening. Today, under the Eugenic Protection Law, abortion can be performed legally and safely without hospitalization. This keeps it secret.

Third, in the traditional period, "abortion and infanticide were silently accepted and justified by society only in times of natural calamity or as an unavoidable means of survival."[20] Modern Japan offers many individual reasons for abortion, including economic aspirations and preference for small families. Longer ago, responsibility for abortion was shared by the whole community; now it is borne individually and privately.

Also, while people of past eras distinguished spirits of adults and children, modern Japanese do not. Finally, traditional society did not bury children under seven in a grave. Children were not considered full-fledged members of society. They remained nameless, along with aborted and stillborn children, and were thought to have another chance to be reborn.

In contemporary Japan, however, children, including stillborn babies, have been "humanized." They are buried with adult funeral rites and given posthumous Buddhist names as full-fledged family members. A major problem emerges with aborted children--when there is no ceremony, there is no name. Yet with "the perspective of the Japanese concept of life and spirits, the aborted child in contemporary society should have a name."[21]

To summarize, traditional, communal society did not cause the individual to bear the burden of abortion or infanticide alone. In the more private, modern experience, the emotional burden is placed

uniquely on the individual. The breakdown of communal support for sufferers is a key to analyzing emotional reaction to abortion in contemporary Japan.
Smith writes,

> In our research on *mizuko kuyô* we have come to realize that what is of central importance in any analysis of non-relatedness or broken connection in Japan is the steady deterioration of traditional ancestral bonds. This cannot be overemphasized.[22]

Within the current context of humanization of the child, anxiety about *mizuko* curse, and privatized suffering with loss of traditional support, *mizuko kuyô* emerges as an attempt to create, repair, and maintain connections with the child lost in abortion.

Mizuko Kuyô

Now we will examine the term *mizuko kuyô*. *Mizuko* is written with characters meaning literally "water child or children." The term has been used since the Tokugawa period for aborted, miscarried, and stillborn infants, babies who die soon after birth, and victims of infanticide. Today the word usually refers to artificially aborted babies but also includes any early death, up to about age seven. *Kuyô*, a Buddhist concept that means literally "to offer and nourish," originally meant "the giving of alms to a priest for the benefit of the dead."[23] Now it means consolation rites for the dead.

Mizuko kuyô affects women and men of all ages, socio-economic levels, and denominational lines--from within established Buddhism to new religions. Miura claims that the appeal of *mizuko kuyô* extends even to Christians.[24] *Mizuko* rites can be offered only once or regularly--daily, monthly, or yearly. *Mizuko* rites can be observed privately or in a group, for an individual *mizuko* or as part of a service for multiple *mizuko*.

Shiunzan Jizoji in Chichibu (Saitama prefecture) west of Tokyo is a temple founded in 1971 expressly for the practice of *mizuko kuyô*. I visited this temple, commonly known as Mizuko Jizoji, in early February 1990, the day after a rare snowstorm in Tokyo. No one else was around. Even without activity, the tier upon tier of more than twelve thousand snow-frosted Jizo statues with their red bibs and whirling pinwheels was an awesome sight.

This mass display includes individual recognition. The family's prefecture is carved on the front of the base of each statue. The family's name, varied in specifics, and sometimes the date are carved on the side of the base. Statues are available in three sizes and costs: Y230,000 ($1800) for the eighty-five centimeter one, Y180,000 for sixty-five centimeter, and Y150,000 for fifty-five centimeter. They can be ordered and paid for by mail. In addition to the initial expense, Shiunzan Jizoji charges an annual maintenance fee of Y5000. Earlier, the temple operated on contributions.

Shiunzan Jizoji advertises services beyond providing *kuyô* for aborted and miscarried infants. It works to create societal trends for checking abortion and offers general counseling. The temple keeps the grounds clean, supplies pinwheels and flowers, changes bibs on a regular basis, and provides special seasonal decorations for festivals such as March girls' day and May boys' day. A peaceful, pleasant environment for the *mizuko* being prayed for is maintained.

Grief and Healing

Both Eastern *kuyô* and Western grief therapy recognize that abortion involves sorrow at a deep psychic and spiritual level. For this, healing is required. Buddhist priest Miura Domyo writes,

> ...the actual existence of the *"mizugo"* [sic] will always nag at the parents' conscience and the mother who shared her body with it as well as the father, of course, can never forget the *'mizugo'* as long as they live. In fact, by neglecting it, a source of evil will remain with the couple, their children and grandchildren.[25]

Pioneer, Christian grief therapists Dennis and Matthew Linn and Sheila Fabricant state, "When we deny our eternal relationship with any deceased member of our family, something tugs at us from the next world asking to be recognized."[26]

Both *mizuko kuyô* and prayer therapy are forms of ritual that provide support. Smith notes, "The pain of grieving, inevitably personal, becomes more bearable when it can be shared, when it becomes less private."[27] *Mizuko kuyô* outwardly entails prayers for the soul of the aborted, miscarried, or stillborn child and consolation for the mother and other family members.

Smith analyzes *mizuko kuyô* as a kind of ritual of affliction in which personal and societal problems are recognized and interconnected.

> Again and again our research reveals how frequently women in Japan, in seeking explanations for repeated illnesses, financial troubles, or tensions within the family begin to attribute these to an earlier experience of

abortion. This search for causation is entirely understandable.[28]

This is also found in Western thought, not just in what Brooks calls non-rational, non-scientific Japanese thought.[29]

Is the ritual of *mizuko kuyô* helpful? Can the traditional ritual and cosmology of a Buddhist temple provide comfort for modern Japanese women and men? Japanese still live with portions of traditional worldviews. The worldview addressed with *mizuko kuyô* still satisfies and comforts them. The importance of doing the ritual is not surprising to one who knows how Japanese culture performs *kuyô* for everything from used sewing needles or calligraphy brushes to dolls to undeliverable mail. Surely, humanized infants also deserve proper rites.

Within religious and cultural contexts, both *mizuko kuyô* and prayer therapy's aim is to console and heal, both the living and dead. Either can deepen faith. Although *mizuko kuyô* can be a one-time act, at places such as Shiunzan Jizoji, it emphasizes an ongoing relationship with the lost child. This is consistent with the Japanese worldview of active relationship between the living in this world and the dead in another world.

Hashimoto Tetsuma, head priest of Shiunzan Jizoji, makes a poignant point for maintaining this relationship, in addition to personal and temple prayers with Jizo statues. To atone for not having the expense of raising the child, one hundred yen should be offered at the family altar for each *mizuko* each day. The shortcut of offering one large sum once a month is not to be taken. Just as things are offered daily for a living child, so should this be done lovingly and willingly as an apology to the *mizuko*. This money can then be donated to the temple or used for pilgrimage.[30]

Reference was made to the counseling services offered at some temples that perform *mizuko kuyô*. In addition to the consolation rites, temple personnel teach about future lifestyle. They "stress that consolation rites are ineffective without repentance."[31] Twelve-Step-like support groups have emerged at some temples. Some temples provide notebooks for women to write about their experiences. Through sharing, they find support. They realize they are not alone in their suffering and grief.

Of course, *mizuko kuyô* is not always authentic. Sensational, commercial motives and unscrupulous priests exist. *Mizuko kuyô* practice can invoke either sincere religious experience or a grasping for an easy solution or quick fix. It can manifest both rich doctrine and ethics or empty ritual. In a positive way, *mizuko kuyô* shows Japanese

Buddhism adapted to distinct, current need and genuine concern for human relationships. More negatively, *mizuko kuyô* can be a mere, hasty "patch up" to avoid underlying issues.

Thus, to evaluate the effectiveness of *mizuko kuyô*, broader issues involved must be weighed. Both widespread abortion and the *mizuko kuyô* phenomenon indicate greater societal malaise. In addition to healing abortion trauma, family or societal hurts that cause abortion also need attention.

On one level, through *mizuko kuyô* thousands of women are being helped with passing through the mourning process after experiencing the turmoil of abortion. That certainly has great value. On the other hand, there remains a need to address the specific factors which keep making abortion so frequently necessary. These are rarely being addressed.[32]

In addressing the problems that create the abortion/*mizuko kuyô* issue, the Christian church has been negligent. Christian faith and theology should own and address this. The Christian church should develop better ways to care for those broken by the experience of abortion. For this, it can learn much of value from *mizuko kuyô* when practiced well.

Mizuko kuyô takes a firm stand that something must be done about the life and relationships broken through abortion. *Mizuko kuyô* acknowledges that something important has happened. *Mizuko kuyô* provides opportunity for shared grief. *Mizuko kuyô* gives consolation through ritual and ongoing relationship. The Christian church dare offer no less in its care.

Works Cited
1 Smith 1988:3
2 Hoshino and Takeda 1987:314
3 Smith 1988:4
4 *Ibid.*,5
5 Coleman 1983:17
6 Young 1989:32
7 Miura 1983:14
8 Brooks 1981:137
9 *Ibid.*
10 Hoshino and Takeda, 313
11 Coleman, 4

12 *Ibid.*, 17
13 *Ibid.*, 30
14 Smith, 8
15 Young, 33
16 Brooks, 133
17 *Ibid.*, 134
18 Hoshino and Takeda, 316
19 *Ibid.*, 313-15
20 *Ibid.*, 313-14
21 *Ibid.*, 315
22 Smith, 19
23 Brooks, 119
24 Miura, 31
25 *Ibid.*, 15
26 Linn, Linn & Fabricant 1985:133
27 Smith, 7
28 *Ibid.*, 15
29 Brooks, 134
30 Tetsuma 1985:199-200
31 Young, 36
32 Smith, 22

A good friend of author Beyler, Japanese professional artist Kazuaki Saitou, honored her in 1986 by sculpting her head in bronze.

Bibliography

Brooks, Anne Page. 1981 "*Mizuko Kuyô* and Japanese Buddhism," *Japanese Journal of Religious Studies*, 8/3-4:119-47.

Coleman, Samuel. 1983 *Family Planning in Japanese Society: Traditional Birth in a Modern Urban Culture*, Princeton, NJ:Princeton University Pr.

Hashimoto Tetsuma. 1985 *Mizuko Jizoji Reigen Shu* [*Mizuko Jizoji Miraculous Efficacy Collection*], Tokyo:Shiunso.

Hoshino Eiki and Takeda Dosho. 1987 "Indebtedness and Comfort: The Undercurrents of *Mizuko Kuyô* in Contemporary Japan," *Japanese Journal of Religious Studies*, 14/4:305-20.

Linn, Dennis, Matthew Linn, and Sheila Fabricant. 1985 *Healing the Greatest Hurt*, New York:Paulist Press.

Miura Domyo. 1983 *The Forgotten Child*, Nuffield:Aidan Ellis.

Smith, Bardwell. 1988 "Buddhism and Abortion in Contemporary Japan: *Mizuko Kuyô* and the Confrontation with Death," *Japanese Journal of Religious Studies*, 15/1:3-24.

Young, Richard Fox. 1989 "Abortion, Grief and Consolation: Prolegomena to a Christian Response to *Mizuko Kuyô*," *The Japan Christian Quarterly*, 55/1:31-39.

15

"...the plane tree's kind to the poor dull city—
I love [it] best of all." **Edith Nesbit**

From Riches to Rags...
Development in Bangladesh

Sharon L. Miller

Bangla, the Golden

Bangladesh lies in the delta of three of the world's greatest rivers--the Brahmaputra, the Ganges, and the Meghna. Rich silt flows down through the rivers, creating a dark alluvial soil which is among the most fertile in the world. Tropical temperatures and abundant rainfall create an ideal climate for agriculture. Crops are grown twelve months a year. The numerous rivers and ponds produce an abundance of fish. The United Nations Food and Agriculture Organization reports, "Bangladesh is possibly the richest country in the world as far as inland fishery resources are concerned." (FAO Brief, 1973)

With a population of 120.86 million (1993), it has the eighth largest population of any country in the world, in an area of 143,998 km (the size of U.S. state Wisconsin). The country's dense population bears testimony to its rich agricultural base. As one Bangladeshi scholar remarked, "There is probably no other society in the world in which such a heavy population can subsist on the land without destroying the resource base." (Maloney, 1986)

A 1976 Senate Committee on the Judiciary reports that Bangladesh "is rich enough in fertile land, water, manpower and natural gas for fertilizer not only to be self-sufficient in food, but a food exporter, even with rapidly increasing population size." (Hartmann, 1982) This has been possible because of 1) the unique, rice-growing, peasant culture which has adapted to the land and 2) the Bangladeshi social organization which has evolved over the centuries.

Bangladesh, once known as "Bangla, the Golden," is known as the world's "basketcase." Life expectancy at birth is only fifty years;

one of every four children does not live beyond the age of five. The infant mortality rate--125.0 per thousand live births--is among the highest in the world. A 1989 Population Crisis Committee study ranked the status of women in ninety-nine countries worldwide. Based on life expectancy, mortality rates, age of marriage, contraceptive use, education, literacy and employment rates, the status of women in Bangladesh is ranked lowest in the world (Wilson-Moore, 1989).

The initial blow to this area came through British colonialism-- the land was robbed of resources, privatized, and consolidated within the hands of the rich. People were taxed into poverty. The rescue attempt by western development projects has exacerbated the division between social and economic classes, increased the number of poor, landless peasants, and furthered the oppression and poverty of women. The reasons for this negative effect can be found in the unexamined presumptions and definitions of "development and progress."

The Development Legacy

> Science that does not respect nature's needs and development which does not respect people's needs will threaten the survival of both. (Shiva, 1988)

After the legacy of colonialism, when the blatant exploitation of "under developed" countries was no longer acceptable, development programs sought to help these countries "catch up with the west." The idea of development is built upon the assumption that western style progress is possible, and indeed desirable, for all. This was not a sudden altruistic move on the part of the industrialized west, but a desire to expand the market for their manufactured goods. For multinational corporations, it was an acceptable way to exploit cheap labor and gain access to raw materials. The sales job was well done; development programs were viewed as "gifts" from the west. And the belief was held that given time and money, the less developed countries would catch up.

Women were often used as the *raison d'etre* for many of the development projects. Progress would provide them with a higher standard of living, more labor-saving devices, healthier children, education, and health care. Some believed that the improvement of women's economic wellbeing would flow automatically from the expansion and diffusion of the development process. By the end of the decade, there was evidence that in many cases development was the problem and women were the victims of modern technology.

Women bore the costs of development but were excluded from many of the benefits. Although the process impoverished large numbers of men, women tended to lose more. The concentration of land into plantations or large farms displaced women more critically. Expansion of cash crops undermined food production. Women were often left with little to support their children, the aged, and the infirm--those who have always been their responsibility.

Within the development mindset, all work that does not produce a profit or capital is seen as nonproductive work. Traditional societies and women's work are viewed as primitive and inefficient unless they are developed or modernized. Thus in the 1974 census on Bangladesh the majority of women were viewed as "inactive."

With a total of 31.6 million women living in the rural areas of Bangladesh, twenty million were considered to be potentially part of the work force. Of these, 15.5 million were listed as "housewives," 3.5 million as "inactive" and only seven hundred forty thousand were "employed" (i.e. in the paid work force) while twenty-six thousand were "looking for (paid) work." Employment figures like these are extremely misleading. In 1984-85 the National Labour Force reported that seventy-eight percent of males were employed and only eight percent of females.

The widespread involvement of women in economic activities is not taken into consideration. Most of this takes place within the village or the homestead, due to the rules of *purdah* (seclusion). These restrictive laws which "protect" women from the view of men are imposed most strictly on middle income women. Wealth allows a degree of flexibility for a few, and poverty exerts a force of necessity on other women.

The village *mullah* (religious teacher) and the men in positions of wealth (therefore power) in the village use the issue of *purdah* to bring women into line and to control their movements within the village and labor force. If a woman ventures too far into the public sphere, (and if her employment threatens the employment of men in the village) her reputation is called into question. She risks ostracism within the village. Very poor women are driven out of their homes in search of paid labor and therefore must risk the social stigma attached to them. Because of these restrictions, women's work is primarily within the village limits, often behind their home's fence or wall.

Much of this labor is not grounded on an income-generating basis. It involves barter with neighbors plus the production of food and materials used within the family unit. If a woman does engage in some small cottage industry (raising poultry, making quilts or fishnets, etc.), she must give these items to a household male to take to market, where she is not allowed. Thus, a woman's involvement with economic activity, on a macro level, seems minimal. What she does or makes does not affect the Gross National Product; economists, development theorists, and World Bank easily dismiss her contribution.

A breakdown of a rural woman's responsibilities will show, however, that the services she performs are crucial for family maintenance and, indeed, for the country and economy as a whole. Five main areas of income-generating production exist for women in rural Bangladesh: grain production; jute production; tree, vine and vegetable cultivation; animal husbandry; and craft manufacturing. To illustrate the involvement of women in one area that is typically seen as a "male domain," note the following breakdown of tasks for the production of rice (paddy), the main crop of Bangladesh:

a. Field operations--land preparation, transplanting, weeding and harvesting done mainly by men. Very poor, landless women are beginning to be hired as day laborers in transplanting, however.

b. Threshing--carried out jointly by men and women. Women gather and stack the straw, after threshing, and dry the straw for fodder.

c. Winnowing and sieving--carried out exclusively by women. Both operations must be done several times.

d. Drying--carried out by women. Grain must be dried at least three times during the process. Grain is dried in the courtyard, which must be guarded at all times from birds and animals. The grain must be turned at regular intervals.

e. Parboiling--done exclusively by women. A very time-consuming operation, fuel must be collected and the paddy boiled in large drums over slow fires.

f. Husking, polishing, milling--done exclusively by women. This is very labor-intensive work.

g. Storing--(domestic and market stocks of rice and seed) traditionally women's work.

h. Marketing--done exclusively by men. Since men have planted the crop and ultimately take the crop to market, it is seen as a male crop. (Chen, 1986)

Women also share in the production of jute, wheat, and winter crops of mustard, millet, and lentils. Women are the sole workers in the cultivation of fruit trees, vines, and vegetables. Although rice is the main crop of the country and the main element in a Bangladeshi's diet, these small house gardens provide people with at least a minimum of protein and vitamins. All care of animals and poultry falls into the women's domain as well. They collect fodder, haul water, milk the cow, and collect dung for composting or fuel. Women make many of the items that are used in and around the home--from the clay stove they cook on, bamboo trays to winnow rice, mats to sleep on, quilts, jute macrame hangers for storage, etc.

Men erect the walls and thatch the roofs of huts, but women help lay the foundation and regularly resurface the floors with a mixture of mud and dung. Women also slice and weave the bamboo from which walls of the house are constructed and fences made. Women (and children) collect firewood, collect and dry dung for fuel, fetch water from a communal pond or near-by river, and prepare meals for the household.

Rural women work on average fourteen hours per day--as much as four hours more per day than men. During rice processing season, women may work up to nineteen hours per day on the paddy. But because they are usually not engaged in cash-earning enterprises, the census considers most of them to be "unavailable" for work or "nonworking" housewives! The World Bank (1987) has admitted that women's contributions to income-earning activities is about half the rate for men, and that eighteen to thirty-two percent of the women are in the economically active population. Even this is too low an estimation, given the reality of most women's lives.

The reason so much of women's labor has been discounted is because it is primarily for the sustenance of the family and not for profit.

> From the perspective of Third World women, productivity is a measure of producing life and sustenance; that this kind of productivity has been rendered invisible does not reduce its centrality to survival--it merely reflects the domination of modern patriarchal economic categories which see only profits, not life. (Shiva, 1988, 5)

Work which meets needs and ensures survival is devalued and discounted.

The Green Revolution Legacy

The Green Revolution was meant to usher in the new age of agriculture. Miracle seeds, developed by scientists in the west, would produce bumper crops. These would feed the population and even allow for exports of surplus, which in turn would bring in much-needed foreign currency. Begun in the 1960's, the new high-yield crops did show immediate promise of alleviating hunger and ending chronic food shortages in many less developed countries. Within twenty years, however, reality showed some of the shortcomings of this erstwhile miracle, and in some countries there was actually a decrease in overall grain production or nutritional levels.

In Bangladesh the vast majority of farmers are poor. According to 1978 figures, forty-nine percent of the agricultural land was owned by the richest ten percent of the population and only two percent of the land was owned by ten percent of the smallest land owners. Most farmers have less than three acres of land. This is often divided into smaller parcels, distributed among villagers. These farmers found themselves increasingly marginalized, as a result of new agricultural methods and high yield seeds that wealthy farmers used. They had no access to credit or political influence (both of which were necessary to obtain irrigation and fertilizer); they could not compete against the larger, wealthier farmers.

Further marginalized, poor women had no access to money and credit; they could not even go to market. The traditional crops grown by women--primarily pulses and greens--accounted for a good deal of the nutritional diet of Bengalis. With the introduction of new, high-yield crops, pulses and grains were increasingly replaced with single rice crops. Land that had been used to produce food for family consumption was converted to produce crops for sale and profit. This created a further split between male cash crops and the survival economy supported by women.

Also hurt was animal production, another responsibility of women. The new high-yield rice had much shorter stalks, which meant that there was less fodder for animal feed. In areas of Bangladesh where the new seeds were used, the animal population decreased markedly. This resulted in less manure, an important source of fertilizer since it maintained moisture in the soil and the worm population. Dried manure was also used as fuel for cooking stoves; women therefore had to go further afield in search of firewood. This in turn resulted in deforestation of areas. Fewer cattle also meant less milk for consumption by children and the elderly. Again, the women's economy was hurt the most.

The green revolution, designed by multinational corporations and western male experts, homogenized nature's diversity. In the end it threatened even the crops that were supposed to increase. Wealthier farmers, who initially benefited from this agricultural revolution, eventually found themselves with problems too. The new seeds were highly vulnerable to pests and insects; only an increased use of pesticides could maintain the high level of production. The genetic uniformity of the crop meant that the whole crop was susceptible to disease and drought. Farmers became hesitant to take this risk.

The new seeds and the new method of farming also created a dependency on western technology. Traditionally, women had selected and preserved seed to be used for the next crop. Now new seed had to be purchased each year, for hybrid seed does not reproduce itself. Imported fertilizers and pesticides, many derived from petroleum products, needed to be purchased yearly too. New technology did not create a country more able to take care of itself but a country more dependent on outside assistance and foreign aid.

Other forms of modern technology, supplied in many cases by western development projects, also hurt the economy of the poor, particularly women. Mechanized rice processing mills were introduced in the 1970's, lauded as tremendous labor saving devices. In a country such as Bangladesh, however, labor saving devices are usually detrimental to peasants. They merely help the rich get richer.

In the rural economy seventy percent of all rice is husked by women. It provides one of the few paid jobs available to them; it can be done in the privacy of one's own homestead. Mechanical and automatic mills, encouraged by low interest loans from the government and provided by development projects, are gradually taking over the market. While the average mill has a capacity of twenty *maunds* an hour, the average woman's is but one six-hundredth *maund* per hour. The mill is three hundred and thirty times as powerful and day-for-day might displace a comparable number of women.

In 1977 there were seventy-six hundred licensed mills; they were increasing at a rate of five to seven percent annually. This displaced work from an estimated one million two hundred thousand women a year! (Shiva, 1988) Mechanized mills were earning large profits for wealthy farmers at the expense of small farmers who could not afford to have their rice processed at the mills. The small farmer was dependent on the unpaid labor of women within the household.

Many other agricultural extension programs introduced into Bangladesh--such as poultry raising, livestock care, and the fish industry--also hurt the economy of women. Responsibility shifted from women to men. Most western agricultural workers were men. Because of *purdah* rules, they did not have access to women in villages to train them. They also failed to respect traditional cultural definitions of women's spheres of work.

In western cultures farming and fishing or livestock and poultry care are more often defined as male tasks. Western "experts" worked out of the same *modus operandi*. Many of these programs were also dependent on small, start-up loans that were not available to women, since they lacked credit. Poultry and livestock raising and the fish industry had traditionally been small, family-run operations. Now western agricultural workers developed these into industries with men as employees.

Although there has been some recognition of the adverse affects of development projects on women, the cost to them continues to be discounted. The 1987 World Bank study of Bangladesh states,

> Surprisingly little is known about the overall impact of technology changes on women's employment or about what could be done to promote technologies which are more conducive to expanding productive employment for both men and women (166).

The report then goes on to discuss the number of women displaced by rice milling (estimated at two million), displaced in gleaning grain, and in the handloom sector. Although the evidence is there, development and funding agencies obviously do not want to seriously consider alternatives to their western, patriarchal models of progress.

The Status of Women in Bangladesh

Ester Boserup in *Woman's Role in Economic Development* traces the status of women in various cultures throughout the world. Women are respected and valued more in cultures where they are recognized as active participants in the family economy. In many African cultures, women are the ones who till the soil. If a man buys more land to farm, he also must have more wives to work the soil. Because of the value of women in these countries (if nothing more than as additional labor force), wives must be purchased from their families. Although women remain subservient to husbands, they do retain a certain level of respect and autonomy.

In Bangladesh an entirely different situation exists. The contribution of women to the family economy is ignored and discounted. Women are devalued and considered a detriment to the family. Their birth is a time of mourning, not rejoicing. One study found that seventy percent of rural men and eighty percent of urban men believe that women are inferior to men and that motherhood is the most desirable role for a woman (Chaudhury & Ahmen, 1980).

A young girl is considered a burden and expense to her family, for she brings in no wages, and yet must be fed and clothed until marriage. Then a dowry must be paid to the groom's family. Although the legal age for marriage is eighteen years for women and twenty-one for men, the average age for marriage (in 1975) was thirteen for rural girls and fourteen and one-tenth for urban girls. Of females under the age of nineteen, sixty-nine percent were married. Males averaged ten years older. This resulted in many women being widowed at an early age, left to fend for themselves and their children. Few incentives remain to delay marriage for a young girl, as long as the worth of her labor is ignored.

The few development projects with a positive impact on women's lives are those of some of the non-governmental organizations working within Bangladesh. The success of the NGOs has been due to the many-faceted approach embodied. They have helped to organize cooperatives for rural women and small loans. They have provided education--including about contraception, basic health and sanitation--plus immunization for infants and children. This multifaceted approach offers women a new awareness of their situation and knowledge of the choices that are available within their limited lives. It empowers them.

Successful, rural cooperatives have been begun by women trained by the NGOs. These in turn train locally recruited female field staff. Unlike development projects, which are often planned from long distance by "experts," the agenda for each group remains with the women of the cooperative. Some choose to begin to raise poultry while others concentrate on weaving, the production of fishnets, small vegetable gardens, raising goats, etc. Small, start-up loans may be issued to individuals, with the cooperative acting as the guarantor for the loan. The repayment rate for these loans is phenomenal, averaging ninety-eight and four-tenths percent for one lending agency.

The women involved in these cooperatives are the poor and destitute, widows, single mothers supporting children, and landless peasants. These programs will not make them rich in their lifetimes. But they will be enabled to feed their children, provide the bare necessities of health care, and perhaps allow children to attend school for a few years. This is subsistence living--peasants will remain poor. But they will have at least a modicum of self-support and self-respect and will be less dependent on the vagaries of the very limited job market.

Conclusion

There are two kinds of poverty: subsistence living as poverty versus the material experience of poverty that results from dispossession and deprivation. Bangladeshi people have always been poor, but theirs is a poverty of subsistence. Many of the development projects--heralded as the panacea of the country's ills--have resulted in further poverty for the marginalized. Such poverty is the poverty of deprivation and dispossession, which is much worse.

Subsistence economies, which satisfy basic human needs through self-provision, are not poor in terms of being deprived. Yet the ideology of development perceives them as deprived because they do not take part in a money economy or consume market commodities. Thus a bamboo or mud house with a thatch roof is considered inferior to, and more primitive than, a cement house with a tin roof. Hand-made cloth, woven and dyed at home, is considered inferior to that which is commercially produced. Prudent subsistence living is seen as poverty; it legitimizes development projects.

In an attempt to alleviate the culturally perceived poverty, development projects operate. Ironically, many of these projects rob the country's resources and further marginalize the poor, particularly women. The aid programs that have benefited peasants have not sought to radically alter their way of life. Instead, they respect the rich culture and heritage that has sustained Bengalis for generations. Rather than patronize the poor or expect that "they" need to catch up with "us" (the west), these programs recognize that western procedures are not always superior. In fact, they may be detrimental to other's well being.

Bangladesh is poor; it likely will always remain poor. But its people need not live in abject poverty. Theirs is a country rich in beauty and culture, if not in western material goods. Aid programs which respect the autonomy and knowledge of the peasants, and which assist them to attain a subsistence level of life, will in the end be the most successful.

Bibliography

Boserup, Ester. 1970. *Woman's Role in Economic Development.* London:George Allen and Unwin. Ltd.

Chaudhury, Rafiqul H. and Nilufer R. Ahmed. 1980. *Female Status in Bangladesh.* Dhaka:Bangladesh Institute of Development Studies.

Chen, Martha Alter. 1986. *A Quiet Revolution: Women in Transition in Rural Bangladesh.* Dhaka:BRAC Prokashana.

Faaland, Just and J. R. Parkinson. 1976. *Bangladesh: The Test Case for Development.* Boulder, CO:Westview Press.

Hartmann, Betsy and James K. Boyce. 1979. *Needless Hunger.* San Francisco:Institute for Food and Development Policy.

Islam, Shamima, ed.. 1982. *Exploring the Other Half: Field Research with Rural Women in Bangladesh.* Dhaka:BRAC Prokashana.

Kanesalingam, V., ed. 1989. *Women in Development in South Asia.* New Delhi:Macmillan India Limited.

Khandker, Shahidur. 1988. "Determinants of Women's Time Allocation in Rural Bangladesh," *Economic Development and Cultural Change,* 37:111-126.

Maloney, Clarence. 1986. *Behavior and Poverty in Bangladesh,* Dhaka:University Press Limited.

Roy, Manisha. 1975. *Bengali Women,* Chicago:University of Chicago Press.

Shiva, Vandana. 1989. *Staying Alive: Women, Ecology and Development,* New Delhi:Kali for Women.

Wilson-Moore, Margot. 1989. "Women's Work in Homestead Gardens: Subsistence, Patriarchy, and Status in Northwest Bangladesh." *Urban Anthropology* 18 (33-4):281-297.

World Bank Country Study. 1987. *Bangladesh: Promoting Higher Growth and Human Development,* Washington, D.C.

16

*"I'll lie here and learn
How, over their ground
Trees make a long shadow
And a light sound."* **Louise Bogan**

Development, East and West

Lynda D. Nyce

Social theorists and political leaders, both feminist and non-feminist, have studied third world development on a large scale. Feminist theorists have argued that the structural position of women in the third world resembles the position and status of colonies, where the concept of women as a last colony has been used as a metaphor for liberation. In order to work at development among the third world colony of women, some feminist theorists have espoused a gender de-colonization that entails a transformation of power relations between men and women.

The following paper will explain several contemporary perspectives on development theory and then argue that a similar type of analysis must be used to critique contemporary western society. In fact, much can be learned from the advances and struggles of our sisters in third world nations who have sought to develop their own situations.

Development Theory

Development has been a word used to describe the overall concerns and efforts of western or capitalist nations and international organizations towards helping those called the poor in "underdeveloped" countries around the world. Used generically, development often overlooks differences in political structures, class struggles, race relations, and power relations that exist among the "underdeveloped" countries.

But as Sen and Grown (1987, 28-29) have argued, a narrow band of processes bind these countries together, to minimize their differences. These common threads include:

• domestic inequalities of income, employment, land ownership, and control of resources;

- destitution of the population;
- lack of basic survival items such as food, shelter, health care, and other services; and
- an unfavorable place in the world economy.

Common features bring diverse nations together under the term *third world.* (Minh-ha, 1989)

But development efforts have traditionally not emerged from a third world perspective. Most development strategies emerge from views and economic priorities of developed countries. Further, these have been applied across the board, without consideration for national differences and priorities.

Sen and Grown (1987) feel that this has led to "denationalizing" many third world countries. Such a process leads to dependence upon foreign markets and single-item export industry or agriculture. The denationalizing process also purports the idea that men are the primary wage earners and thus should be the foundation of development efforts. Women's productive roles or public roles are excluded from the process.

Much of classical development literature ignores women's economic contribution. It considers women passive dependents who mainly perform reproductive tasks. But in 1970 Ester Boserup established, via empirical study, the vital position of women in economic development and agricultural economics. Boserup also uncovered a division of labor by gender across nations by showing that women's productive work was not reported in official documents or in any development literature.

From colonial through capitalist development literature, Europeans have had little regard for communal and egalitarian relations among the indigenous people they were meant to develop. But research of several pre-colonial societies has revealed equality, not hierarchical relationships, between men and women in productive economic roles. (Etienne and Leacock, 1980)

> The imposition of European patriarchal relationships that presupposed the universal subordination of women in many instances deprived native women of property and personal autonomy and restricted the productive functions and any public roles they might have played prior to colonization. (Acosta-Belen and Bose, 1990, 306)

By imposing a hierarchical, western understanding of social relations and by not validating the communal or cooperative work of women, development agencies created power differentials that have excluded women. They ignored the possibility of egalitarian relationships between women and men.

Recent studies have attempted to abolish the classical development perspective by considering the productive economic role of women and women's collective organization. L. Beneria (1982, 135) emphasized the "need to counteract the ideological underdevaluization of women's work" by including use-value in addition to exchange-value production in defining labor.

Use and exchange-value production refer to processes where the product is for other's use or enhancement without any fee or charge or barter, and where the product is created for exchange with other products or fees, respectively. [The terms and meanings are originally from Karl Marx in *Das Kapital*.] Beneria terms the whole range of women's activities as "ways of making a living," instead of "ways of earning a living" in order to include daily survival activities undertaken by women.

Women's Organizations

Studies that emphasize the inclusion of all aspects of women's work in development efforts have increased global awareness of the rising scope of women's poverty. Throughout the world, development and governmental officials express concern for the "feminization of poverty." Yet, poor women in the third world increasingly call attention to their strengths. They use their responsibilities as workers and mothers to enter both formal and informal economic markets and as a base for political demands. Their stories and advances can also serve as a guide to fight the effects of a "feminization of poverty" in the United States and Europe.

Workers in developed countries struggle for survival on a daily basis within a global system replete with

* erratic growth,
* increased conflict and competition,
* decreasing wages,
* a greater gap between the rich and poor, and
* a greater number of marginalized citizens.

In many ways these features parallel those found in "underdeveloped" countries. Since parallels exist, a logical place to turn for alternatives to partisan political reform is to our sisters who have, for many years, struggled for daily survival against the colonization of the west.

According to June Nash, (Nash, 1983) the majority of Latin American women have acted against the collapse of their subsistence economy by organizing collective meals, mothers' clubs, neighborhood water-rights groups, health cooperatives, and craft collectives which produce goods for local and international markets. Instead of privatizing daily survival issues, these women collectively form social-change groups for economic and social survival.

Transforming women's roles has been advanced in India and Bangladesh by establishing lending organizations or banks which grant small loans to women in order for them to begin a business. Many of these banks, such as SEWA (Self-Employed Women's Association) in Ahmedabad, Gujarat, India, have had repayment rates of 94-99 percent. Such success must be attributed to the investment in personal and collective advancement which instills in participating women a sense of community and self worth.

Helen Safa (Safa, 1978) argues that as the public-private split becomes negligible in women's lives, collective action then targets the state in order to demand running water, electricity, transportation, and basic human rights. Traditionally, Safa states, women (third world) have avoided partisan politics because it continues to be a male sphere that rarely speaks to women's issues. By addressing women's issues of daily survival, women can organize for change or utilize existing organizations to transform women's roles.

Los Angeles

During the 1990s, events in the economic and social atmosphere in the United States have called attention to the need for transformation of women's roles and racial relations. The work of contemporary feminist development theorists can be helpful to such needed transformation. So can the examples of women in third world nations.

During the second week of May in 1992, riots (revolt) raged through the streets of Los Angeles, California. The impetus for the turmoil was the acquittal of four white police officers charged with beating an African-American man while trying to arrest him. Racial injustice capped off an environment ready to explode.

South central Los Angeles has characteristics parallel to third world countries:

• decreasing wages,
• lack of access to resources,
• an increasingly poor and marginalized population, and
• high unemployment.

These mitigating factors caused the city to erupt with anger and outrage.

The task to rebuild the city continues--a task previously not considered a priority by elected officials. They have spent limited time among inner city inhabitants to understand the culture and reality present there. When faced with the job of developing the city, officials find themselves caught with a colonial, dependence-theory or view of the culture of south central Los Angeles.

Once again, leaders may be tempted by a classic idea of rebuilding the city to meet their own economic priorities and issues, rather than to allow those who live in the area to develop their own reality. Few leaders willingly promote lending agencies similar to those developed in India and Bangladesh, to encourage people in Los Angeles to invest in their personal and community development.

But in light of the immense success that third world banks have achieved with "less educated, underdeveloped" persons, how can this alternative be ignored? By allowing and encouraging women and men in Los Angeles to focus on daily survival issues in order to develop themselves, the advances made by collective women's organizations elsewhere could benefit the socially and economically segregated United States.

Homelessness

Problems such as homelessness and extreme poverty have long been associated with the third world and with women. Yet, as Los Angeles has shown the western world, no longer can these issues be neglected from consideration in all areas of the globe. Mother Teresa claimed that poverty in the United States was worse than poverty in India.

Even though poverty remains acute in countries such as India, many people share a commonality in their poverty. In the United States, the poor, while forced to live amidst one of the most affluent nations in the world, are viewed by many as bums, failures, drug addicts, alcoholics, and societal rejects. This atmosphere leads to low self-esteem, isolation, and often to a loss of hope.

Despite a growing homeless population in the United States, too little help is forthcoming from officials or development agencies. Instead, for example, the federal government slashed funding for programs to assist the homeless to $17 million in 1992-1993, a decrease of over $70,000 from just four years prior. A few organizations across the country actively work to instill in homeless people respect and dignity for themselves and to provide needed life skills training. Yet, these organizations stress the need for people to help themselves rather than to assist through cooperative efforts.

Talking and interacting with homeless persons leads to the hypothesis that, given a chance, many would like to work together in developing themselves. Frequently, people mention the support and friendship of other homeless people as the most important ingredient in trying to put their lives back together. At the South Bend (Indiana) Center for the Homeless [where I worked among Center guests as a graduate student intern] cooperative efforts and communal ties arise from the daily struggle of homeless persons to find jobs, raise their self-esteem, and put their lives back together.

Women living at the Center note the importance of others. In a sharing session, three women spoke of their backgrounds and experience at the Center. Judy commented,

> I didn't think anyone cared. And then to know someone cared and wanted to give me something was great. I also realized that other people here have more problems than I. The people here let me talk. Listening to other guests makes me realize other people have problems greater than I. I really want to follow the "straight and narrow," get my G.E.D. [high school diploma equivalency] and be independent.

Sandy echoed Judy's message:

> For a long time I've known I'm an alcoholic. Now I'm going to AA [Alcoholics Anonymous] discussion groups. People here let each other talk; people like Mike greeted me and made me feel at home. I want to get sober.

Lori, 21, has straightened out her life.

> I am a recovering alcoholic and drug addict. The first time I was here I couldn't have cared less about myself or what I was doin'. I'd go out, but came back when I didn't have nowhere to stay; something made me come back here. Nobody puts you down here, no matter how bad things in your life have been. Without Karen, I don't know what I would've done. I'm not as angry anymore. There are a lot of times you don't fit into a program here. If you demonstrate to others you don't care about yourself, they'll do the same to you. But I'd just like to say that this place and the closeness of the people really help. We're like family. This place has been a great

support without this place to come to, who knows where I'd be.

Once a month people of the Center meet together for a "community meeting." Staff members often use the occasion to inform guests of the Center's financial reality and to report upcoming events. Then time is given to questions from the guests. But an April 1992 meeting that I recall included a "pitch for community" from the staff; it elicited a positive response from the guests.

Margie began the meeting by saying, "This is a community, your house. Keep it clean."

Tim then gave the following appeal.

> We gotta help each other out, be community to each other, check up on each other. We've not been doin' enough here (all of us, staff, guests and volunteers) to really help each other out. If you want just to get by, this is not the place for you. We must have the courage to work hard and not give up. We need leaders to emerge from you people sitting here. We need people to check on others and say, "If you don't have the courage to change, walk." We can't be soft on ourselves; we can't give up even though society is not behind us. We need to identify leaders, people who want to "take the bull by the horn." Too many people have given up. If you are interested in not just talking about this, challenge others quietly or loudly. This is the only way we can be better.

Numerous responses followed this appeal. The first came from Rick. He said he does "help people in lots of ways. We got to start somewhere, let people know you work hard and have a positive attitude. If you ask me to help you out, I will."

Another male said, "Staff haven't gone through the situations that people here have. That's why people come to me, because I've been through it and am surviving."

To these comments Tim added, "It's important to have role models here, someone to say you screwed up, but be compassionate also. Failure comes often; you have to hang in there and try to work at it."

Rick again spoke, "We should be glad to help out here. My family has a place to stay; my family's not out on the street. Come time

to eat, everybody's in line but come time to clean up and everyone leaves. That ain't fair."
Once again Tim spoke:

A better staff wouldn't make a difference if you don't want to help yourself.
[Rick interjected, "A stricter staff would make it worse."]
Unless we address these problems frankly, we won't change. Love has to be tough in order for something to change; you all deserve it. We are far from perfect, so keep check on staff also. So be compassionate to each other. Concentrate on yourselves but help others. Only through community and care can we make changes. The reason we're talking to you is because we care about you and you deserve better.

During the meeting, no women spoke of their concerns or their value for community. But when asked to name ideas and projects, such as organizing a Center daycare rotation, the women valued community and cooperation.

Conclusion

In conclusion, women across the globe who struggle to meet the daily survival needs of themselves, their family, and their community have been able to achieve "development" via organizing for the collective goal of their neighborhoods or social class. Recent development theories, especially those of feminist theorists, have valued the collective process and advocate increased collective efforts in the third world. Yet most theorists have been hindered from suggesting that such efforts are necessary to combat the increasing unrest and stratification in developed nations.

But the social realities of the poor and marginalized in the west demand consideration of programs already known to help women and men in third world nations. The incentive toward collective efforts can be glimpsed in some pockets of developed nations. That inclination needs to be nurtured and encouraged via the programs and example of third world sisters and brothers who have taken development into their own hands. God help us in "developed" nations to learn from those we have often considered "less developed."

Bibliography

Acosta-Belen, Edna & Christine E. Bose. "From Structural Subordination to Empowerment, Women and Development in Third World Contexts," *Gender and Society*, 4/3, Sept. 1990, pp. 299-320.

Beneria, Lourdes, ed. *Women and Development: The Sexual Division of Labor in Rural Societies*, NY:Praeger, 1982.

Boserup, Ester. *Women's Role in Economic Development*, NY:St. Martins, 1970.

Etienne, Mona and Eleanor Leacock, eds. *Women and Colonialization: Anthropological Perspectives*, NY:Praeger, 1980.

Minh-ha, Trinh T. *Women, Native, Other: Writing Postcoloniality and Feminism*, Bloomington:Indiana University Press, 1989.

Nash, June and Maria Patricia Fernandez-Kelly, eds. *Women, Men and the International Division of Labor*, Albany, NY:SUNY Press, 1983.

Safa, Helen. *Women in Class Society*, NY:Monthly Review Press, 1978.

Sen, Gita & Caren Grown. *Development, Crises, and Alternative Visions*, NY:Monthly Review Press, 1987.

ANNOTATED BIBLIOGRAPHY

Dorothy Yoder Nyce, Editor

Biographies enrich; they influence those who follow after; they teach as surely as do scriptures. To women who cry, "We know so few mentors," a reader might reply read ten good biographies! To women who have never learned to read, who are blind, who do not have access to a library, or who lack the luxury to spend money for books, readers will be sensitive.

Perhaps you have read several of the following: Raj (India) by Gita Mehta, *The Joy Luck Club* (China) by Amy Tan, *Feminine Ground* (Tibet) edited by Janice D. Willis, *May You Be the Mother of a Hundred Sons* (India) by Elisabeth Bumiller. To tell others how what you learn from women writers and characters helps makes sense of your own life further extends the value of story.

In case readers of this collection wonder what to read next, the annotations that follow offer a few options from global settings. These could be imaged as vibrant flowers or tasty fruit. Beyond roots, trunk, and branches, think of these as buds, as diverse berries to admire or savor, or as autumn colored leaves—all worthy features of trees around us.

Carver, Ann C. & Sung-Sheng Yvonne Chang, eds. *Bamboo Shoots After the Rain - Contemporary Stories by Women Writers of Taiwan*, NY:Feminist Pr, 1990.

Fourteen stories, divided by three generations, make up this fine collection. It incorporates tradition and modernity, plus conflict and respect toward each. Brief introductions to both author and story are helpful. Political history shapes more early writers born on the mainland and younger ones in Taiwan.

Content varies: one woman guards the fact that she is an undertaker; another struggles to learn to whistle; a widow and widower reach for companionship; panic about disrespect toward Chairman Mao surfaces. Cultural features abound. Writing style varies. One writer forces the reader to keep alert to time shifts; one intersperses very long paragraphs with conversation of staccato marks.

With editors from two nations, this resource includes an essay that asks, "Can One Read Cross-culturally?" With good effect, the question is illustrated through a story where a wife and concubine live within one household. The book's purpose of introducing English-language readers to representative literature by Chinese women from Taiwan is indeed achieved.

----

deJesus, Carolina Maria. *Child of the Dark The Diary of Carolina Maria deJesus*, Trans. from Portuguese by David St. Clair, NY:New American Library, 1962 (with multiple reprints).

Reading this, one gets a vivid picture of the struggle to survive within a slum in Brazil (or wherever slums thrive). The years covered are 1955-59. Mother of three children (Father's Day is a ridiculous idea.), Carolina wrote about life on bits and pieces. She sensed the value of recording experience; she did not know how to sleep without "reading."

Named by reviewers the main "character" of the book, hunger hounds throughout. Ironically, I read this book soon after a novel about royal family experience; in that account a word that recurred was power. Here bread, dream, nervous, and complaint recur--between jaunts to scrub clothes and count *cruzeiros* for scrap paper or iron gathered. Predestined to pick up things (except happiness), Carolina was also racially black.

She understood rebellion; not so the Brother come to preach. They also differed on who should have children, the rich or poor. Religion caused arguments in the *favela* as did lack of privacy, thieves, and overhearing. "A woman's tongue is a candlewick. Always burning." Yet, woman is crucial.

"January 1, 1960. I got up at 5 and went to get water."

Fogelklou, Emilia. *Reality and Radiance Selected Autobiographical Works of EF*, Into. and Trans. by Howard T. Lutz, Richmond, IN:Friends United Pr, 1985.

This resource introduces Fogelklou's long life, from 1878-1972. The first Swedish woman to complete a theology degree, "Mi's" spirituality sustains this content. Although a teacher at different times in her life, her lecture circuits and published works were even more influential. I would hope to read her biography of Sweden's St. Birgitta.

Readers find insight into friendship, Fogelklou's childhood, and the discovery that she "was already Quaker." In her relatively short marriage with Arnold Norlind, they profoundly share elements of nature, the world of Dante, and "living" with death. Radiance of spirit is real; nuggets like "A human being is a path" occur to ponder.

Gmelch, Sharon. *Nan The Life of an Irish Travelling Woman*, NY:W
    W Norton & Co, 1986.

Before reading this, I was unaware of the meaning of *Travelling* in the subtitle. To learn about Irish culture beyond the conflict between Protestants and Roman Catholics proved refreshing. But the hardship endured was no less real. Anthropologist Gmelch listened and observed with care.

This account about a Travelling Woman, of the category known as gypsies or "tinkers," clarifies their pattern of existence. Nan retells her life--1919 to 1983--made more authentic, in part, through the simple technique of the pronoun *me*. Her family survives, in part, through equally simple but never easy trades.

With "enough" children the Donahues encounter a gamut of experience: risky births, education, cruelty, fear, transition, omens, deceit, separation, and love. Why Nan sticks with Mick has to do with honor. Why she values the life of a Traveler for herself, but would not wish it for children of hers, makes sense.

Travelers show uncanny strength. They endure judgment from others in society. They "make do" with cart and pony plus minimal supplies under a tin roof. They deal with weather when it occurs. Their expectation for meat in the diet offers more surprise than the amount of drink consumed. But the aftermath of the latter lingers longer.

Joseph, Helen. *Side by Side A Personal Account of One South African
    Woman's Struggle against Apartheid*, First Published by Zed
    Books Ltd., London, NY:William Morrow and Co., Inc., 1986.

Writer of several other books, Helen recorded this while in her 70s, as her autobiography. It focuses her experience of three decades, 1953-83, in an intense liberation struggle. Born in England in 1905, she moved to South Africa in 1931, later retaining only SA citizenship.

Her shift to South Africa, after a short stint in India, could be described as fairly "innocent." She had to be taught to be political. Once taught, she could "do no other." Being white—and seeing the privileges it afforded—caused her shame. But she willingly endured disdain too. Charged for "Communist" (socialist) thought, she confronted the unjust, white system. Her book title rings true; she yearned to work or kneel side by side with the disadvantaged but majority blacks, Indians, and coloured.

From historic protest gatherings to forming interracial organizations of women to presenting speeches, Helen was an activist. This led to being banned four times (up to five years at a time) and "unbanned" in between, jailed (gaoled) four times, and on trial for four years on a charge of treason. How a government can intimidate, incarcerate without trial, and rule by force because threatened becomes clear. How a person with will and strength defies the same is to be applauded.

The ANC's (African National Congress) colors—black, yellow, and green—almost appear in print. Threads of the 1955 Freedom Charter recur in the text; the whole appears as an appendix. A map would have been helpful.

Luo, Zi-Ping. *A Generation Lost China under the Cultural Revolution*, NY:Avon Bks, 1990.

Here, readers find one woman's striking account of her family's story. Accused for his bright, scientific mind, (that officials claimed he used in anti-Revolution effort) the Father was dismissed from a newspaper job and "held hostage" within his own home. The same twenty years found the writer's Mother first in prison then ordered to be a farm worker. Through Xi-ou Tan, the second of four children, the story unfolds.

A series of twenty-five letters, and transition paragraphs that explain, provide the writing format. Xi-ou Tan and her younger brother find a suicide message. The writer of that note, Professor Hu, becomes the recipient of Xi-ou's daily letters--her attempt to convince Hu of life's worth.

Not exaggerated, the account is painfully realistic. Those who aid, believe, and befriend the family are introduced. So too are those who return to search the family's house or otherwise distrust and defame them. Courage and persistence prevail. Family love and loyalty

Annotated Bibliography—Editor 143

pervade. Rarely do readers find the human will for self-education or disciplined recording of insight more convincing. Remembered poetry and philosophy recur. Conversation and prose know balance. Shanghai history (1950's through the '70s) is laid out, map-like. Scheming and deep feeling intersect. I *highly* recommend the book.

Moody, Anne. *Coming of Age in Mississippi The Classic Autobiography of Growing up Poor and Black in the Rural South,* NY:Laurel/Dell Pub, 1968.

Growing up black in the US south was tough during the '40s and '50s. Confronting racism in the '60s was even tougher. But Anne Moody did both. Chapters follow chronology--from childhood through high school and college--with gradual readiness for activity within "The Movement."

From being unfairly charged for starting a fire in her childhood home to being pictured on the Klan "wanted" list, Moody struggled. As a young domestic worker, she knew who believed in her, who did not. She saw how a few murders worked to intimidate the many. She knew the agony of trying to get her people to trust efforts for voter registration. And after years of exhaustion, she could only wonder when hearing the next generation sing, "We shall overcome."

The family and church, the community and police, the co-workers and opponents all enter in strategic ways. So do poverty, and the determination to find a job or the agony of raw hunger. An intelligent student and tireless worker, Anne would not take "ignore it" for the answer to injustice. She embodies the truth through candor, hope, and wisdom, in spite of fear and threats. Courageous!

Selby, Bettina. *Riding to Jerusalem*, NY:Peter Bedrick Bks, 1985.

A fine combination of geography, history, and culture comes together in this account of Selby's 1984 solo bike trip from London to Jerusalem. Actually, the four thousand miles on Evans (the bike) goes from London to Venice and from Istanbul to Jerusalem, with a ship trip in between on the Adriatic, a portion of the Mediterranean, and Aegean Seas. From late July through mid-December, in spite of intense heat, several rainstorms, and vigorous terrain, Selby rides and reports.

Selby had planned well, route and supplies. Not her first five-month venture, 1982 had found her biking from Kathmandu to Karachi. An appendix details the reliable bike (not a flat tyre throughout) plus her belongings stored in panniers. Where and how she found lodging enroute, contacts with people and foods, and informed accounts of pilgrims or Crusaders before her enrich the book. So do vivid descriptions of place and event. Maps were valuable.

Expect adventure, reflection, and determination enough to inspire any fifty-year-old mother of three. Expect wisdom, knowledge, stamina, freedom, and trust. Herself a woman of privilege, Selby's sensitive insight into women of more deprived experience recurs. What a journey effectively told!

Shaaban, Bouthaina. *Both Right and Left Handed Arab Women Talk about Their Lives*, Bloomington:Indiana Univ Pr, 1991.

This resource of interviews with a Syrian author portrays experience in Syria, Lebanon, Palestine, and Algeria. The aim is to improve the lot of Arab women through an honest highlighting of their struggles and aspirations. To define dignity and respect matters when talking about equality.

Those interviewed include students, the wife of a long-term PLO prisoner, and leaders of women's organizations. Varied Muslim groups plus a Christian and a few Sahara tribal people find voice. Women's views of their men recur; men reveal expectations about women's emancipation or self-sacrifice. Conversations between generations prove to be interesting too. Differences of opinion surface about sexual equality. Effects of revolution become clear. Efforts for survival receive due perspective, compared to thoughts about sexuality and freedom. Few think that western or European women could be overall more advantaged.

Views and information seem more vital than a striking writing style. In fact, description is rare. Yet the plight of Palestinian women becomes clear anyway, like the pain of forgetting the dearest. At times the shift between interviewer and interviewee begs for more clarity, and the title poses enigma. But the book certainly warrants reading.

Soon, Cho Wha. *Let the Weak Be Strong A Woman's Struggle for Justice*, Lee Sun Ai and Ahn Sang Nim, eds., Bloomington, IN:Meyer Stone Bks, 1988.

Here is an account of Korean Cho Wha Soon's life. A pastor activist, she effectively integrates priestly and social action. Short chapters detail content division. In between the years of her comfortable growing up and current experience appear sections that detail pastoral ministry, industrial mission work, and "witness." The last was vital to what preceded it too.

Eighteen years' work with UIM (Urban Industrial Mission) is key to understanding Cho Wha Soon. More difficult than to pastor, confronting the labor system activated her "pastoring heart." She engaged God or recalled scriptures when faced with tough situations: when healing a possessed person, nudging demonstrators, betrayed, under surveillance, or repeatedly interrogated and imprisoned.

Cho Wha Soon knew the values of being trained, of training others. Countering weakness, she insisted on strength. Several who knew her conclude:

> Having experienced the unconscious putdown by male colleagues...and marginalization for being involved in social justice ministries, especially involving women, she has a deep sensitivity to women's feelings and status in church and society.

Spindel, Carol. *In the Shadow of the Sacred Grove*, NY:Vintage Books, 1989.

Village life in West Africa's Ivory Coast is described through the experience of a privileged American who lived there most of a year. To gather agricultural research, Tom settled among the Senufo and Dyula people several months before Carol joined him.

As the title suggests, the sacred grove (place of ancestors) serves as the book's recurring thread--its mystery, its exclusion and threat, its power. *Power* pervades experience beyond the ritual of *poro* too. Creative power belongs innately to women. Bush spirits pervade. Powerful magical knowledge may be inherited by or granted to a special elder. And power affects the routine of giving blessings--for a night ahead, overdue rains, or a personal health crisis.

Here parades sensitivity to culture followed by the reward of being included. Trust is established and broken. Research must continue but not at the expense of time for funerals, weddings, or birthing events. The importance of learning language precedes linkage with women potters. Privacy gives way to the villagers' lining the "living room" bench. At the same time, Tom and Carol's relationship becomes public. He also cooks; she is not beaten; nor does she become pregnant. Often generous, their access to food during a spartan, dry season stalks the western couple.

For a fine glimpse into village life--whether through the work of diviners or termites--enjoy this book, attentive to women's experience.

Contributors

The well is deep from which these contributors write.

Women's experience worldwide "waters" or enriches the task of doing theology. Women's experience provides the essential moisture for the graphic trees of life to provide stability and beauty. From their deep or shallow roots to stark yet stretching branches, trees can symbolize the complex and the sacred in women's lives.

Elizabeth Soto Albrecht was born in Puerto Rico. After serving as Assistant Secretary for Latin America and the Caribbean with Mennonite Central Committee, Akron, PA, she served in Bogota, Colombia from 1993-1996, in part as Dean of the *Seminario Biblico Menonita* and Director of CLARA, a publishing venture. She now parents two children at home.

Patricia Zapata Barco, born in Bogota, Colombia, is married and the mother of four children. A free lance writer and journalist who creates book designs, she also works with human rights—with refugees and women's issues--and with NGO's in Colombia.

Kathy Bergen (Her article identifies her, prior to her assignment as National Coordinator of Middle East Peace Education with American Friends Service Committee, Philadelphia, PA.)

Mary Beyler has served in Japan since 1974 with Mennonite Board of Missions. During her assignment in Kitami, Hokkaido, she did this research on *mizuko kuyô* for a seminary course in folk religions. Another Japanese cultural interest is tea ceremony, which she has studied for more than ten years.

Rachel Hilty Friesen is a pastor and historian. With her husband, Ivan, she serves as co-pastor of Oak Hill Mennonite Church in Winston-Salem, North Carolina. She is a graduate of Toronto School of Theology (Th.M. in Church History). The Friesens are parents of three adult children.

Jean Gerber, mother of four, lives in Belgium. She has worked for more than a decade in a library for children in which she specializes in peace education.

Judy Zimmerman Herr, with an MDiv degree from Pittsburgh Theological and mother of two sons, works as Secretary for the Overseas Peace Office of Mennonite Central Committee. She previously spent nine years working with her family in Southern Africa under MCC.

Mary Yoder Holsopple, a graduate of Associated Mennonite Biblical Seminary, Elkhart, IN, and mother of two children, worked with MCC for three years in Uganda in community work with women and for seven years in Swaziland and Mozambique in administration. Currently from Goshen, IN, she manages a school-based program in violence intervention.

Gayle Gerber Koontz taught at Silliman Divinity School in the Philippines for two years in the late eighties. With a Ph.D from Boston University School of Theology, she is Professor of Theology at AMBS, having been Academic Dean and for one semester Interim President. She is co-parent of three children.

Mary Kay Burkhalter Larson served for thirteen years with her husband Jonathan in Botswana, with the General Conference Mennonite Church. Both grew up in India and served together with MCC in Zaire. Parent of three children, her doctoral studies at Johns Hopkins University focuses population dynamics. Her current position of epidemiologist is in the division of reproductive health at the Centers for Disease Control and Prevention in Atlanta, GA.

Melanie A. May is Dean of the Program in the Study of Women and Gender in Church and Society and Professor of Theology at Colgate Rochester Divinity School/Bexley Hall/Crozer Theological Seminary. An ordained minister in the Church of the Brethren denomination, she is active in National and World Council of Churches Faith and Order work. Her writing includes: *Bonds of Unity: Women, Theology and the Worldwide Church*, being editor of *Women and Church: The Challenge of Ecumenical Solidarity in an Age of Alienation*, and most recently *A Body Knows A Theopoetics of Death and Resurrection*.

Sharon L.Miller, daughter of missionaries, lived in India, Pakistan, the Philippines and Bangladesh until age nineteen. With an MDiv. degree from McCormick Seminary, Chicago, she is currently finishing her PhD in Sociology of Religion at the University of Notre Dame, IN.

Dorothy Yoder Nyce, editor of this book, is from Goshen, IN. She is parent of two adult daughters and a DMin. Graduate of Western Theological Seminary, Holland, MI (Project: *Dialogues to Foster Interreligious Understanding*). Her current, two-year, seminary assignment with the Evangelical Lutheran Church in America in Chennai, India combines programming in areas of inter-religious dialogue and women's studies. She previously edited *To See Each Other's Good*—a complement to this collection of stories about global women—*Weaving Wisdom Sermons by Mennonite Women;*and *Which Way Women?;* in addition she wrote *Jesus' Clear Call to Justice* and *Strength, Struggle, and Solidarity: India's Women*. Committed to cooperative effort, experience includes media/video projects, volunteer work with boards of international agencies, a Fulbright-funded study tour in India titled "Women, the Family, and Change in India," living in India for other periods of time, and many friendships across cultures over four decades.

Lynda D. Nyce is currently Assistant Professor of Sociology at Bluffton College in Ohio. She is completing her PhD. dissertation, which focuses on homelessness, at the University of Notre Dame, IN. Notre Dame alumni awarded her as Distinguished Graduate Student for combining acedemics with community involvement. She has lived short-term in India and China plus volunteered one summer with Hispanic children in San Antonio.

Janet Umble Reedy recently from Holland, MI, and mother of two adult daughters, has lived in Asia for over nine years--working with the Mennonite Central Committee in Indonesia, Thailand, and Vietnam. For three years, the Reedys administered MCC projects in agriculture, primary health care and education in Hanoi. They recently returned to Indonesia—this time to lead the Goshen College Study Service Term.

Manini Nayar Samarth taught English at St. Mary's College, Notre Dame, IN prior to her current role of lecturer in English at Penn State University, State College, PA. She has written fiction for periodicals in the U.K. and India and stories for the BBC World Service. Among her awards are the Margaret Church Prize for short fiction from Purdue University and first prize in STAND magazine's 1991 International Story Competition.

Lisa Schirch earlier coordinated Native Concerns for MCC Ontario. At present Assistant Professor in the Conflict Transformation Program at Eastern Mennonite University, Harrisonburg, VA, she concurrently is a PhD candidate in Conflict Analysis and Resolution at George Mason University.

Laurel Voran, a freelance artist, was graduated from Goshen College with a degree in art and natural science. She enjoyed hiking in Nepal and several months of volunteer work with the Sisters of Charity and the Women's Development Centre in Calcutta, India, in 1991. A recent graduate of the Longwood Professional Gardner Training Program, she looks forward to a gardening internship in England.

Linda Witmer is a friend of both of the Kekchi women about whom she writes. She has worked for over ten years in Guatemala with the Kekchi Mennonite church--serving with Eastern Mennonite Mission and Mennonite Central Committee.